JUAN RODULFO

Fortune Cookie Coaching

88 Motivational tips made of fortune cookies, Vol. I

First published by Aussie Trading 2024

Copyright © 2024 by Juan Rodulfo

All rights reserved. No part of this publication may be reproduced, stored or transmitted in any form or by any means, electronic, mechanical, photocopying, recording, scanning, or otherwise without written permission from the publisher. It is illegal to copy this book, post it to a website, or distribute it by any other means without permission.

This novel is entirely a work of fiction. The names, characters and incidents portrayed in it are the work of the author's imagination. Any resemblance to actual persons, living or dead, events or localities is entirely coincidental.

Juan Rodulfo asserts the moral right to be identified as the author of this work.

Juan Rodulfo has no responsibility for the persistence or accuracy of URLs for external or third-party Internet Websites referred to in this publication and does not guarantee that any content on such Websites is, or will remain, accurate or appropriate.

Designations used by companies to distinguish their products are often claimed as trademarks. All brand names and product names used in this book and on its cover are trade names, service marks, trademarks and registered trademarks of their respective owners. The publishers and the book are not associated with any product or vendor mentioned in this book. None of the companies referenced within the book have endorsed the book.

First edition

Cover art by Guaripete Solutions

*This book was professionally typeset on Reedsy.
Find out more at reedsy.com*

Part of the profit from the sale of this book is used to help dozens of families suffering from the Humanitarian Crisis in Venezuela, and at the same time is collaborating with the spread of the truth about Crimes Against Humanity and Human Rights violations, Venezuelans suffer daily and are overshadowed by the propaganda apparatus of the misnamed "Bolivarian revolution."

Contents

Preface		iv
1	Riches	1
2	Frugality	3
3	Style	5
4	Sense of humor	8
5	Limites	10
6	Exciting destination	12
7	Center of attention	14
8	Enhance your feminine side	17
9	Take chances	20
10	Help a friend	23
11	Treasure your good memories	25
12	Feed yourself well	28
13	Spending	31
14	Random Act of Kindness	34
15	Path to success	37
16	The usefulness of a cup	40
17	Politeness cost nothing	42
18	Simple Kindness	45
19	Knowledge and ignorance	48
20	Do your best	51
21	Some fortune cookies	54
22	No need to worry!	57
23	Desert sands	60
24	Get things done	63
25	Necessity	66

26	Understanding	68
27	Desire is explosive	71
28	Vacation	73
29	Family reunion	76
30	The daily grind	79
31	The calling	82
32	Solutions	84
33	Strength	87
34	Improve finances	89
35	Smiling	92
36	Wondrous opportunity	95
37	The dice	98
38	Tomorrow	101
39	Un sourire	104
40	Dark room	106
41	New possibilities	109
42	Darkness	112
43	Superior person	114
44	Taxes and fines	117
45	Friendship	120
46	Real estate and stocks	123
47	Success	126
48	Passionate relationships	128
49	Right doors	130
50	Simplify your life	133
51	Take chances	135
52	The rainbow and the rain	138
53	Bounded by the Sky	141
54	Successful in Business	143
55	Investment opportunity	145
56	Love and happiness	147
57	Beauty	149
58	Equals	151

59	Trust others	154
60	Error and truth	157
61	Cooperative people	160
62	Original ideas	163
63	The effect you have	165
64	Your goals	168
65	A banker	170
66	Marketable ideas	173
67	Education, knowledge and action	176
68	Write a letter	179
69	Good spirits	182
70	Award	184
71	New and different	186
72	Always on our minds	188
73	Plans	190
74	Prosper	192
75	Respect for others	195
76	Definition of life	198
77	Visit a park	201
78	Spirit of adventure	203
79	Purpose and direction	205
80	Follow your heart	208
81	The evening	210
82	Good luck	212
83	You are beautiful	214
84	Be what you are	216
85	Happiness	218
86	Financial life	220
87	Convictions	222
88	Influential people	224
About the Author		227
Also by Juan Rodulfo		229

Preface

Welcome to Volume I of "Fortune Cookie Coaching: 88 Motivational Tips Made of Real Fortune Cookies". This book is a culmination of a 13-year journey, part of three volumes, a collection of wisdom tucked inside those delightful little cookies we often receive at the end of a meal in Chinese restaurants.

Over the years, I've found myself captivated by the simplicity and profundity of these messages—small slips of paper containing insights that resonate deeply with human experience.

As I sifted through my collection, I couldn't help but notice the recurring themes of luck, fortune, and positive energy—themes deeply rooted in Chinese culture, where colors and numbers hold significant meaning and are believed to bring good fortune and prosperity. It's fascinating to consider the impact of these cultural beliefs on our perceptions of luck and success, and how they shape our actions and attitudes in life.

These small, crisp cookies, often served at the end of a meal in Chinese restaurants, have been a source of joy and surprise for many. Hidden within each one is a slip of paper bearing a message, a prophecy, a piece of advice, or a glimpse of some truth about life. Over the years, I have collected these pearls of wisdom, and they have served as a source of motivation and inspiration, not just for me, but for many others.

In Chinese culture, colors and numbers have significant meanings and are often associated with good luck. Red symbolizes good fortune and joy, while the number 8 is considered the luckiest number because it sounds like the word for wealth or fortune. In this book, I have incorporated these elements of Chinese culture to enhance the richness of the experience. Each motivational tip, each nugget of inspiration, is carefully chosen to bring you a lucky dose of wisdom.

But this book is more than just a collection of fortune cookie messages. It is a testament to the power of motivation and inspiration in shaping our lives and our world. I firmly believe that when we are motivated and inspired, we can achieve great things. We can overcome challenges, we can reach our goals, and we can make a positive impact on the world. More importantly, motivation and inspiration can help to reduce evil in humanity by encouraging positive actions and promoting understanding and empathy.

Learn Chinese — honey
蜂蜜　　*feng mi*

Beyond cultural symbolism, I've also come to realize the transformative power of motivation and inspiration in our lives. In a world often plagued by negativity, fear, and uncertainty, the messages contained within these fortune cookies serve as beacons of hope, guiding us towards a brighter, more optimistic future. They remind us of the inherent goodness within humanity and inspire us to rise above our limitations, to embrace our potential, and to pursue our dreams with unwavering determination.

You might be wondering: can motivation and a good fortune cookie message truly impact the world? The answer is a resounding yes. Negativity and cynicism, like shadows, can dim our potential. But with a spark of inspiration, a flicker of belief in ourselves and each other, we can illuminate a path towards a brighter future. This book aims to be that spark, that gentle nudge towards reducing the "evil" in the world – not through grand gestures, but through the quiet power of self-improvement, positivity, and empowered action.

This book was written in part using Artificial Intelligence (AI). AI has been a valuable tool in organizing and presenting the material in a meaningful and engaging way. But more than that, AI represents the positive evolution of humanity. It is a testament to our ingenuity and our relentless pursuit of knowledge and understanding. With the help of AI, we can solve complex problems, make informed decisions, and create a better future for all.

Now, you might also be curious – how does Artificial Intelligence find a place in fortune cookies? This book is a unique collaboration between human intuition and the ever-evolving world of AI. The insights you'll find within are gleaned from real fortune cookies, but the organization, analysis, and presentation have been guided by the powerful tools of AI. This synergy is a testament to the positive evolution of humanity. Just as fortune cookies themselves are a fusion of Eastern and Western traditions, this book reflects how AI can collaborate, not replace, human creativity and wisdom.

Lucky Numbers 34, 35, 31, 53, 21, 25

As you delve into the pages of this book, I hope that you will find motivation and inspiration in its contents. May the wisdom of fortune cookies guide you on your journey, and may you find the riches that life has to offer.

In crafting this volume, I enlisted the help of Artificial Intelligence—a tool that has become increasingly integral to our lives and our understanding of the world around us. With the assistance of AI, I was able to distill the essence of these motivational messages, harnessing their power to uplift, inspire, and empower readers on their own journeys of self-discovery and personal growth.

But perhaps most importantly, this collection serves as a testament to the positive evolution of humanity—one in which technology, like AI, plays a pivotal role in shaping a brighter, more inclusive future for all. As we navigate the complexities of the modern world, it's heartening to see how technology can be harnessed for good—to amplify our voices, connect us with one another, and empower us to create positive change in the world.

So as you embark on this journey through "Fortune Cookie Coaching: 88 Motivational Tips," I invite you to open your heart and mind to the wisdom contained within these pages. May these messages serve as guiding lights on your path, illuminating the way forward and inspiring you to embrace the fullness of life with courage, resilience, and boundless optimism.

Fortune Cookie Coaching: Volume I is just the beginning. There are two more in the oven. As you crack open each page, savor the message within. Let it be a catalyst for personal growth, a reminder of your immense potential, and a nudge towards a brighter future – for yourself and the world around you.

Before you dive in, be aware that the book is also a YouTube Channel and a Podcast, available in most of Podcast players and its website: fortunecookie.coach

With warm regards, The Author

☺ Your are beautiful in and out. People see this. ☺
14   19   32   40   47   6

1

Riches

There are riches headed your way.

Dear readers of "Fortune Cookie Coaching",

I want to share with you a phrase that I recently found in a fortune cookie: "**There are riches headed your way**". This simple sentence carries a profound message of hope, optimism, and anticipation. But what does it truly mean?

Riches are not just about material wealth. They are about the abundance of life in all its forms. They are about the wealth of knowledge, the wealth of experiences, the wealth of relationships, and the wealth of personal growth.

So, when we say, "There are riches headed your way", we are not just talking about financial prosperity. We are talking about a life filled with purpose, passion, and fulfillment. We are talking about a journey of self-discovery and self-improvement. We are talking about becoming the best version of yourself.

Remember, the path to these riches is not always easy. It requires hard work, dedication, and perseverance. It requires you to step out of your comfort zone, to take risks, and to face your fears. But rest assured, every step you take, every challenge you overcome, brings you closer to these riches.

So, embrace this journey. Embrace the struggles, the failures, the setbacks. For they are not obstacles, but stepping stones to your riches. They are opportunities for growth, for learning, for becoming stronger and wiser.

And most importantly, believe in yourself. Believe in your abilities, your potential, your worth. For you are capable of achieving great things. You are capable of attracting these riches into your life.

So, dear readers, as you turn the pages of this book, remember the phrase from the fortune cookie: "There are riches headed your way". Let it inspire you, motivate you, and guide you on your journey to a richer and more fulfilling life.

With warm regards, Your Personal Coach

12 20 33 40 42 43

2

Frugality

You shouldn't overspend at the moment. Frugality is important.

Fortune Cookie Fam, listen up! Today's message might sound like a downer, but trust me, it's wrapped in financial wisdom: **"You shouldn't overspend at the moment. Frugality is important."** Don't worry, Fortune Cookie Coaching isn't here to make you feel deprived. It's here to help you build a strong financial foundation, and sometimes, that means taking a step back.

Here's the thing: overspending can be a sneaky thief, robbing you of your financial security and hindering your ability to achieve your goals. But fear not, **frugality isn't about deprivation, it's about mindful spending.** It's about getting the most out of your hard-earned cash.

So, how can you embrace frugality without feeling like you're missing out? Here are some tips straight from Fortune Cookie Coaching:

- **Track your spending:** Awareness is key. Know where your money goes so you can identify areas to cut back.

- **Differentiate between needs and wants:** Ask yourself, "Do I truly need this, or do I just want it?" Prioritize essential expenses like housing and food.
- **Embrace free and low-cost activities:** There's a world of fun waiting outside the mall! Explore nature, visit museums on free admission days, or gather with friends for a potluck.
- **Challenge yourself to DIY:** Can you cook more meals at home? Learn to repair clothes? Develop your skills and save money in the process.
- **Shop smart:** Compare prices, utilize coupons, and avoid impulse purchases. Remember, the best deals aren't always the loudest.

Frugality can be a powerful tool for achieving your dreams! Here's how:

- **Save for your future:** By spending less, you can allocate more money towards your goals, whether it's a dream vacation, a down payment on a house, or a secure retirement.
- **Reduce financial stress:** Knowing you're living within your means gives you peace of mind and allows you to focus on what truly matters.
- **Empowers smart financial choices:** Frugality builds a foundation for future investments and allows you to make informed financial decisions, with the knowledge that your future self will thank you.

So, Fortune Cookie Fam, don't fear frugality! **Embrace it as a powerful tool** for achieving your financial goals and building a secure future. Remember, Fortune Cookie Coaching is here to guide you every step of the way. Go forth, spend wisely, invest in your dreams, and **watch your financial security blossom!** You've got this!

3

Style

YOU HAVE A CAPTIVATING STYLE ALL YOUR OWN.

Esteemed readers of "Fortune Cookie Coaching,"

Today, let us celebrate the artistry that resides within each of you—the brushstrokes of your uniqueness, the rhythm of your authenticity. The universe whispers: **"You have a captivating style all your own."**

1. **The Canvas of Individuality**: Imagine existence as a grand gallery. Each of you hangs a canvas—a self-portrait. Your strokes—bold or delicate—tell stories. Your palette—vibrant or muted—expresses emotions. Your style—captivating and unrepeatable—draws eyes. Embrace your canvas; it's a masterpiece in progress.
2. **The Symphony of Quirks**: Your style isn't a monologue; it's a symphony. The quirks—the offbeat notes—are what make your melody unforgettable. Perhaps it's the way you laugh, the way you wear mismatched socks, or the way you find beauty in raindrops. Play on; the universe applauds.
3. **The Dance of Confidence**: Style isn't about labels; it's about confidence.

When you wear your uniqueness like a crown, you become magnetic. The room leans in; the stars adjust their orbits. You—bold, unapologetic—ignite constellations.

4. **The Haiku of Silence**: Sometimes, style isn't loud; it's a haiku—a few syllables that echo eternity. Your silence—the pauses between words—speaks volumes. It says, "I'm here, fully." The universe leans closer; it hears your whispers.
5. **The Fashion of Kindness**: Kindness is your couture. When you compliment a stranger, when you hold the door, when you listen without judgment—you're dressed in kindness. It's a timeless style; it never goes out of fashion.
6. **The Footprints of Originality**: Originality isn't a trend; it's a legacy. You're not a copy; you're an original print. Your footprints—the ones you leave on hearts, on conversations, on sunsets—are your signature style.
7. **The Cosmic Catwalk**: Picture a cosmic catwalk—the Milky Way as your runway. Walk it with flair. Your scars—the constellations on your skin—are your accessories. Strut; the galaxies applaud.
8. **The Quantum Wardrobe**: In quantum physics, particles exist in multiple states until observed. You, too, have a quantum wardrobe—endless possibilities. Tomorrow, wear courage; the universe notices.
9. **The Encore of Evolution**: Style evolves. Yesterday's trends become today's vintage. Embrace change; it's your stylist. Adapt, experiment, surprise yourself. The universe loves a style chameleon.
10. **The Final Applause**: As we conclude, remember: You're not just a reader; you're a co-author. Your style—the ink on these pages—shapes the narrative. Write boldly; the universe reads every word.

"You have a captivating style all your own." – Unknown

May your brushstrokes be vivid, your rhythm syncopated, and your gallery infinite. ☆🎨

STYLE

6 10 18 20 34 48

Lucky numbers

4

Sense of humor

YOUR SENSE OF HUMOR IS APPRECIATED IN ALL SITUATIONS.

Fortune Cookie Fam, gather 'round! Today's message is a gift wrapped in a sweet treat: **"Your sense of humor is appreciated in all situations!"** Believe it or not, Fortune Cookie Coaching champions this sentiment. Yes, building wealth and achieving goals are important, but laughter? Priceless!

Life throws its fair share of curveballs, and let's face it, sometimes the best way to deal with them is with a good laugh. Here's why your **sense of humor** is a superpower:

- **Stress Buster:** Laughter is a natural stress reliever. It lowers cortisol levels, boosts your mood, and helps you maintain perspective.
- **Connects with Others:** A shared laugh builds rapport, fosters teamwork, and creates a more positive work or social environment.
- **Enhances Resilience:** Humor helps you bounce back from setbacks. It allows you to see the lighter side of challenges and find the strength to keep moving forward.

- **Boosts Creativity:** A playful mind is a creative mind. Laughter can spark new ideas and help you approach problems from a different angle.

So, how can you leverage this amazing talent? Here are some tips:

- **Don't take yourself too seriously:** Lighten up, poke fun at yourself, and don't be afraid to laugh at life's little absurdities.
- **Find the humor in everyday situations:** Train your mind to spot the funny side of things, even amidst challenges.
- **Be mindful of your audience:** What makes you laugh might not have the same effect on everyone. Adapt your humor to the situation.
- **Use humor to diffuse tension:** A well-timed joke can lighten a tense moment and put everyone at ease.
- **Remember, laughter is contagious:** Spread the joy! Share funny stories, watch a comedy, or simply smile at someone.

Fortune Cookie Coaching isn't just about financial success; it's about living a fulfilling life. And trust me, a life filled with laughter is a richer, more satisfying one.

So, Fortune Cookie Fam, go forth and **embrace your inner comedian!** Use your sense of humor to navigate life's ups and downs, connect with others, and create a more joyful existence for yourself and those around you. Remember, laughter is the best medicine – and in the pursuit of your goals, a little dose of humor can go a long way!

LEARN CHINESE - Taste

口 (kǒu) 味 (wèi)

Lucky Numbers 54, 12, 43, 30, 17, 16

5

Limites

 Vous n'avez pas de limite.
2 3 32 35 46 47

Chers lecteurs du "Fortune Cookie Coaching,"

Aujourd'hui, je vous invite à lever les voiles de vos croyances, à briser les chaînes de l'auto-limitation. La phrase qui nous guide est un mantra cosmique : **"Vous n'avez pas de limite."**

Laissez-moi tisser ce discours avec des fils d'étoiles :

1. **L'Horizon Infini** : Imaginez un ciel sans frontières, une mer sans rivage. Votre potentiel est cet horizon. Les étoiles vous murmurent : "Étendez-vous." Vous n'êtes pas borné par les contours de votre peau ; vous êtes un univers en expansion.
2. **La Danse des Possibilités** : La vie est une piste de danse. Vos pas ne sont pas pré-écrits ; ils sont improvisés. Vous pouvez virevolter, sauter, tournoyer. Les étoiles applaudissent chaque mouvement. Dansez, sans retenue.
3. **Le Mythe des Plafonds** : Les plafonds sont des illusions. Vous n'avez pas

de limite de hauteur. Si vous rêvez de toucher les étoiles, construisez une échelle d'audace. Grimpez. Les étoiles applaudissent chaque échelon.

4. **L'Étoffe des Rêves** : Votre esprit est un métier à tisser. Les fils sont vos pensées. Tissez des rêves, des constellations. Les étoiles vous guident. Vous n'avez pas de limite de fil.
5. **Le Feu Intérieur** : Votre âme est une étoile en fusion. Elle brûle d'aspirations, de créativité. N'éteignez pas ce feu par la peur. Alimentez-le. Les étoiles dansent avec vous.
6. **L'Équation Quantique** : La science dit : "L'observateur influence l'observé." Vous êtes l'observateur de votre vie. Votre regard crée des probabilités. Les étoiles applaudissent chaque choix.
7. **Le Silence des Étoiles** : Écoutez. Les étoiles ne parlent pas fort, mais elles murmurent des secrets. Elles disent : "Vous êtes infini." Écoutez ce silence. Il est rempli d'étoiles.
8. **L'Étoile Polaire** : Trouvez votre étoile polaire intérieure. Elle guide vos nuits sombres, vos tempêtes. Elle dit : "Avance." Vous n'avez pas de limite de direction.
9. **L'Univers des Possibles** : Demain, vous serez le centre d'attention. Les étoiles vous observeront. Quelle histoire raconterez-vous ? Osez. Les étoiles applaudiront.
10. **L'Applaudissement Éternel** : En conclusion, souvenez-vous : Vous êtes une étoile parmi des milliards. Brillez. Votre lumière résonne à travers l'éternité.

"Vous n'avez pas de limite." – Inconnu

Que votre voyage soit stellaire, vos rêves infinis et votre courage sans bornes. ✨

6

Exciting destination

Pack your bags. You're bound for an exciting destination.
10 13 18 29 30 45

Fortune Cookie Fam, buckle up! Today's message isn't just a prophecy, it's a call to action: **"Pack your bags. You're bound for an exciting destination!"** Now, this fortune cookie isn't talking about a specific place on a map. It's talking about an incredible **journey of personal growth and transformation**. Remember, Fortune Cookie Coaching is your guide on this adventure!

Life is a magnificent expedition, and sometimes we get stuck in the rut of routine. This little message is a nudge to **break free, embrace the unknown, and embark on a thrilling voyage of self-discovery.**

What exciting destination are you bound for? Maybe it's finally launching that business idea, mastering a new skill, or simply becoming a more confident and empowered version of yourself. Whatever it is, **let the excitement fuel your journey!**

Here's how you can transform this fortune cookie message into action:

- **Define your destination:** What do you want to achieve? What does your ideal life look like?
- **Plan your route:** Develop a roadmap with small, achievable goals that lead you towards your ultimate destination.
- **Pack your essentials:** Equip yourself with the knowledge, skills, and resources needed to navigate your journey. Fortune Cookie Coaching is packed with tools to empower you.
- **Embrace the adventure:** Don't be afraid of unexpected detours, embrace them as opportunities to learn and grow.
- **Celebrate the journey:** Acknowledge your progress, no matter how small, and enjoy the process of becoming your best self.

Fortune Cookie Coaching isn't just about the destination; it's about the **transformative journey** itself. As you embark on this exciting adventure, remember:

- **Growth often lies outside your comfort zone:** Dare to step outside your bubble, explore new experiences, and challenge yourself.
- **Learning is a lifelong adventure:** Never stop acquiring knowledge, honing your skills, and expanding your horizons.
- **Resilience is key:** Obstacles are inevitable, but they don't have to derail your progress. Learn from setbacks, adjust your course, and keep moving forward.

This fortune cookie message is a sign that you are ready for something incredible! Pack your bags, Fortune Cookie Fam! Fill them with determination, optimism, and the wisdom gleaned from Fortune Cookie Coaching. Your most exciting destination yet awaits. Go forth, be bold, embrace the adventure, and **create a life that is truly extraordinary!**

7

Center of attention

> *You will soon be the center of attention.*

Esteemed readers of "Fortune Cookie Coaching,"

Today, I invite you to step into the spotlight—the center stage of your own life. The universe whispers: **"You will soon be the center of attention."**

Let us unfurl the red carpet of possibility:

1. **The Cosmic Spotlight**: Imagine the cosmos—the grand theater of existence. Stars twirl, galaxies pirouette. And there, in the celestial orchestra pit, you stand—a soloist. The spotlight swings your way. Your cue? Life itself. The audience? Everyone you encounter. Take a bow; your performance matters.
2. **The Dance of Destiny**: Destiny isn't a fixed script; it's an improvisational dance. You're not a mere spectator; you're a choreographer. Soon, the spotlight will find you—on a street corner, in a coffee shop, across a Zoom call. Your steps matter; they ripple through time.

3. **The Art of Presence**: Being the center of attention isn't about ego; it's about presence. When you listen, you're the spotlight for someone else. When you share your story, you illuminate shared humanity. Your presence—the spotlight—creates connections.
4. **The Unexpected Encore**: Tomorrow, you might find yourself in the spotlight—an unexpected encore. Maybe it's a job interview, a chance encounter, or a heartfelt conversation. Embrace it; the universe applauds your readiness.
5. **The Fearful Applause**: Fear whispers, "Hide in the wings." But courage says, "Step forward." The spotlight isn't harsh; it's illuminating. It reveals your strengths, your vulnerabilities. Take chances; the audience—life—cheers you on.
6. **The Soloist's Secret**: Soloists don't perform alone; they're supported by an unseen orchestra. Your spotlight—the attention—comes with an ensemble: mentors, friends, ancestors. They play the music of encouragement. Listen; harmonize.
7. **The Encore of Kindness**: When you're the center of attention, share your encore. Kindness, laughter, encouragement—they're encore performances. The spotlight isn't a solo act; it's a duet with humanity.
8. **The Quantum Applause**: Imagine applause as energy waves—the quantum currency of connection. When you touch hearts, the applause echoes across dimensions. Take chances; the universe applauds.
9. **The Dress Rehearsal of Self-Love**: Before the spotlight finds you, rehearse self-love. Admire your quirks, your resilience. The mirror reflects not flaws, but constellations. You're worthy of the spotlight—always.
10. **The Final Ovation**: As we conclude, remember: The spotlight isn't a burden; it's a gift. Shine, dear reader. Your encore awaits. The universe leans forward, clapping in anticipation.

"You will soon be the center of attention." – Unknown

May your spotlight be dazzling, your encore heartfelt, and your standing ovation eternal. ✨💫

1 4 9 12 14 47

Lucky numbers

8

Enhance your feminine side

You should enhance your feminine side at this time.

Fortune Cookie Fam, gather 'round! Today's message might seem a little cryptic, but don't worry, Fortune Cookie Coaching is here to help you decipher it! Our sweet treat whispers: **"You should enhance your feminine side at this time."**

Now, hold on a second! This isn't about lace and ruffles (unless that's your thing!). It's about **embracing the powerful spectrum of qualities** that make you, well, YOU! Fortune Cookie Coaching champions personal growth, and that often involves tapping into all aspects of yourself.

Feminine energy isn't just about gender; it's about cultivating qualities like:

- **Empathy:** The ability to understand and share the feelings of others.
- **Intuition:** Following your gut feeling and trusting your inner wisdom.
- **Creativity:** The ability to see things from new perspectives and find

innovative solutions.
- **Collaboration:** Working effectively with others towards a common goal.
- **Nurturing:** Taking care of yourself and those around you.

So, how can you enhance these aspects of yourself? Here are some ideas:

- **Practice active listening:** Pay attention to what others are saying, both verbally and nonverbally.
- **Spend time in nature:** Nature has a calming effect and can help you reconnect with your intuition.
- **Explore artistic endeavors:** Whether it's painting, writing, or dancing, unleash your creative spirit.
- **Build strong relationships:** Nurturing meaningful connections strengthens your support system and fosters collaboration.
- **Engage in self-care:** Prioritize your physical and mental well-being so you can better care for others.

Remember, Fortune Cookie Coaching isn't about fitting into a mold. It's about **embracing all aspects of yourself** – the traditionally masculine, the traditionally feminine, and everything in between. This holistic approach to self-development will unleash your full potential and allow you to navigate life with greater confidence and success.

So, Fortune Cookie Fam, don't be afraid to express your full self. Enhance your compassion, creativity, and nurturing spirit. You might be surprised at the positive impact it has on your life and the lives of those around you. **Embrace the power within you, in all its beautiful complexity!** Fortune Cookie Coaching is here to guide you every step of the way. Go forth, be your most authentic self, and experience the joy of living a life rich in all its dimensions!

ENHANCE YOUR FEMININE SIDE

您在事業中獲得非凡的成功。

9

Take chances

Take chances.

2, 9, 13, 42, 48, 52

 OPENFORTUNE

Esteemed readers of "Fortune Cookie Coaching,"

As we gather here, our hearts open like pages of possibility. Today, I present to you a phrase—a whisper from destiny: **"Take chances."**

Let us step onto the tightrope of opportunity, balancing between fear and courage:

1. **The Leap of Faith**: Imagine life as a vast canyon. On one side stands safety—the known, the predictable. On the other side lies the abyss—the uncharted, the uncertain. To cross, you must leap. Take chances. Trust that wings will sprout mid-flight.
2. **The Unopened Doors**: Life offers doors—some adorned with golden handles, others hidden in plain sight. These doors lead to realms of

growth, love, and transformation. But they remain shut until you turn the knob. Take chances; open them. Behind each door, a universe awaits.

3. **The Whisper of Regret**: Regret isn't born from failure; it's born from unopened doors. The "what-ifs" echo louder than any defeat. Take chances, for the whispers of regret fade when you dare to knock.
4. **The Canvas of Possibility**: Imagine your life as a blank canvas. Each chance taken—a brushstroke. The colors blend—mistakes and masterpieces. The canvas isn't meant to stay pristine; it's meant to be painted. Take chances; let your brush dance.
5. **The Serendipity Café**: Picture a café where serendipity serves coffee. Tomorrow, visit. Sit by the window, sip warmth, and watch. The person at the next table—the one reading your favorite book—might hold your chance. Strike up a conversation; the universe loves dialogue.
6. **The Quantum Leap**: Not all chances are equal. Some are quantum leaps—the ones that alter orbits. They're disguised as risks, but they're really portals. When you leap, you don't just cross; you transform. Take chances; become stardust.
7. **The Ripple Effect**: Chances aren't solitary; they're ripples. When you take one, others follow. Your courage inspires a friend, who inspires a stranger, who inspires a movement. The world changes—one chance at a time.
8. **The Dance of Vulnerability**: Taking chances is dancing with vulnerability. It's saying, "I don't know the steps, but I'll move anyway." Vulnerability isn't weakness; it's the heartbeat of courage. Take chances; let your heart waltz.
9. **The Invitation to Adventure**: Tomorrow, adventure awaits. It's disguised as a risk—an invitation to explore. The treasure isn't gold; it's experience. Take chances; collect memories.
10. **The Final Revelation**: As we conclude, remember: Life isn't a spectator sport; it's a participatory dance. The music plays; the floor awaits. Take chances; let your soul pirouette.

"Take chances." – Unknown

May your leaps be quantum, your doors wide open, and your canvas vibrant.

☆ 🎨

10

Help a friend

It is time to help a friend in need.
1 12 20 36 44 47

Fortune Cookie Fam, listen up! Today's message isn't just a sweet treat, it's a call to action: **"It is time to help a friend in need."** Remember, Fortune Cookie Coaching isn't just about building your own wealth and success – it's about fostering strong connections and building a supportive community.

Friendship is a precious thing, and like any investment, it needs nurturing. When a friend is struggling, offering a helping hand isn't just the kind thing to do, it strengthens the bond you share. It shows them you care, and reinforces a sense of mutual support that benefits everyone in the long run.

Think about it - when you're facing a storm, having a friend by your side, offering a shoulder to lean on, or simply a listening ear, can make all the difference. Here's how you can be that friend, the friend your fortune cookie is calling you to be:

- **Be present:** Sometimes, the most valuable thing you can offer is your

time and attention. Listen actively, offer a hug, and let them know you're there for them.
- **Offer practical help:** Depending on the situation, maybe they need help with errands, childcare, or a financial bridge loan. Fortune Cookie Coaching can help you assess your own resources and offer appropriate, responsible support.
- **Empower them, don't enable them:** Don't take over their problems. Encourage them to find their own solutions, and offer your support as they navigate the situation.
- **Be patient:** People heal at different paces. Be there for them over the long haul, offering encouragement and celebrating their victories, no matter how small.

Remember, Fortune Cookie Coaching is your guide to building strong relationships. This book equips you with the tools to be a good communicator, a compassionate listener, and a reliable friend.

Helping a friend in need isn't just about generosity, it's an investment in your own happiness. Strong friendships enrich our lives, offer us support in our own struggles, and create a sense of belonging.

So, Fortune Cookie Fam, answer the call of your fortune cookie! Reach out to a friend in need. Your kindness can make a world of difference, and as you strengthen that bond, you strengthen your own sense of community and belonging. Go forth, **be the friend you wish to have**, and together, build a network of support that uplifts everyone involved. Remember, a community that cares for each other is a community that thrives!

有時稍加忍耐勝過足智多謀的算計

11

Treasure your good memories

Treasure your good memories and you need not worry about ending a banquet.

Esteemed readers of "Fortune Cookie Coaching,"

Today, I stand before you as a guide—a lantern bearer on your path toward well-being. Our lives are woven with threads of choices, and today, we unravel the wisdom behind the phrase: **"Treasure your good memories and you need not worry about ending a banquet."**

1. **The Banquet of Life**: Imagine life as a grand banquet—a table laden with experiences, relationships, and moments. Each dish represents a memory—a flavor imprinted on your heart. Some memories are savory, others sweet. But all contribute to the feast of existence.
2. **The Art of Remembrance**: Memories are like jewels—precious, iridescent. They sparkle in the recesses of your mind, waiting to be polished by recollection. Treasure them—the laughter shared, the sunsets witnessed, the whispered secrets. For in remembering, you

relive.

3. **The Fear of Scarcity**: We fear endings—the banquet concluding, the music fading. But what if I told you that memories defy scarcity? They're infinite. Each smile, each tear, each stolen kiss—they echo through time. When you treasure them, you create abundance.
4. **The Alchemy of Gratitude**: Gratitude transforms memories into gold. When you savor a good meal, you thank the chef. Similarly, when you savor a memory, you thank life. Gratitude is the secret sauce—it turns ordinary moments into extraordinary feasts.
5. **The Bittersweet Farewell**: Banquets end; that's their nature. But memories linger. When you bid adieu to a chapter—a friendship, a season, a love—don't mourn. Instead, celebrate the flavors it left behind. The sweetness of first love, the warmth of shared cocoa—these endure.
6. **The Eternal Banquet Hall**: Picture a celestial hall—a cosmic ballroom where memories dance. Loved ones who've departed, moments that shaped you—they waltz together. When you treasure your good memories, you reserve a seat in this eternal gathering.
7. **The Legacy of Laughter**: Memories are heirlooms passed down generations. Your grandmother's recipe, your father's bedtime stories—they're woven into your DNA. When you laugh, you echo their joy. When you cry, you honor their tears. The banquet continues.
8. **The Empty Plate Fallacy**: We fear empty plates—the void left by lost memories. But here's the secret: Empty plates make room for new courses. When you release what no longer serves you, you invite fresh flavors. Trust that life's chefs have more delicacies in store.
9. **The Banquet of Impermanence**: Impermanence isn't sorrow; it's poetry. The fleetingness of a sunset, the fragility of a snowflake—they're verses in the cosmic banquet. When you embrace impermanence, you savor each bite fully.
10. **The Final Toast**: As we conclude this banquet of words, raise your goblets. Here's to memories—the spices of existence, the wine of the soul. May you treasure them, for they're the legacy you leave behind. And when the banquet ends, may you smile, knowing you feasted well.

TREASURE YOUR GOOD MEMORIES

"**Treasure your good memories and you need not worry about ending a banquet.**" – **Unknown**

May your banquet be rich, your memories abundant, and your heart forever nourished. ☆🍽

3 12 23 33 46 48

Lucky numbers

12

Feed yourself well

*Today's a day to nourish yourself.
Feed yourself well.*

Esteemed readers of "Fortune Cookie Coaching,"

Today, I stand before you as a guide—a lantern bearer on your path toward well-being. Our lives are woven with threads of choices, and today, we unravel the wisdom behind the phrase: **"Today's a day to nourish yourself. Feed yourself well."**

1. **The Sacred Ritual of Self-Nourishment**: Imagine this day as a banquet—a feast laid out just for you. The table is set with moments, choices, and opportunities. Each morsel you consume—whether physical, emotional, or spiritual—shapes your vitality. Today, let's dine mindfully.
2. **The Nutrient of Self-Care**: Nourishment isn't just about food; it's about self-care. Like a gardener tending to delicate blooms, tend to your soul. Sip from the cup of solitude; savor the flavors of laughter. Prioritize rest, movement, and moments that fill your cup.

3. **The Art of Savoring**: Life isn't a race to the finish line; it's a tasting menu. Savor each bite. When you eat, taste the textures, inhale the aromas. When you rest, feel the softness of the pillow. When you connect, listen deeply. Nourishment lies in presence.
4. **The Feast of Gratitude**: Gratitude is soul food. Today, serve yourself a plateful. Savor the warmth of morning sunlight, the embrace of loved ones, the symphony of bird songs. Gratitude isn't a side dish; it's the main course.
5. **The Balanced Plate**: Imagine your life as a plate. What ingredients do you pile on? Balance is key. Greens of purpose, proteins of connection, grains of creativity, and spices of adventure. And don't forget the dessert—joy.
6. **The Forbidden Fast**: Sometimes, we fast from self-compassion. We skip meals of kindness, starve ourselves of forgiveness. Today, break that fast. Nourish your heart with gentleness. Let go of judgments; feast on acceptance.
7. **The Soul's Superfoods**: What feeds your soul? Is it art, music, nature, or solitude? Identify your superfoods—the ones that light up your spirit. Maybe it's a walk in the rain, a handwritten letter, or a dance in the living room. Consume them daily.
8. **The Hydration of Tears**: Tears aren't weakness; they're hydration for the soul. Let them flow. Cry for lost dreams, for unspoken words, for the ache of the world. Tears cleanse; they water the seeds of resilience.
9. **The Mindful Bite**: As you nourish your body, also nourish your mind. Feed it curiosity, wisdom, and wonder. Read a poem, learn a new word, explore a different perspective. The mind thrives on variety.
10. **The Eternal Banquet**: Today isn't an isolated meal; it's part of an eternal banquet. Every sunrise, every heartbeat, every shared laugh—it's all nourishment. So, as you feed yourself well today, remember: You're part of a cosmic feast.

In closing, dear readers, may you dine with intention, savoring each moment. May you nourish not just your body, but your essence. For today's

nourishment becomes tomorrow's vitality.
"Today's a day to nourish yourself. Feed yourself well." – *Unknown*
Bon appétit, my fellow seekers of light. ☆🍽

您在事業中獲得非凡的成功。

13

Spending

Perhaps you've been focusing too much on spending,

Esteemed readers of "Fortune Cookie Coaching,"

Today, I invite you to pause—to step back from the hustle and bustle of life and reflect on a simple yet profound truth: **"Perhaps you've been focusing too much on spending."**

Let us unravel the layers of this wisdom:

1. **The Dance of Priorities**: Life is a grand ballroom, and our choices are the dance steps. Imagine each dollar as a partner in this waltz. Yes, spending is essential—it fuels experiences, meets needs, and brings joy. But when the rhythm becomes frantic, when we chase after every glittering distraction, we lose sight of the true melody—the symphony of purpose.
2. **The Mirage of More**: Society whispers, "More is better." We chase after the latest gadgets, designer labels, and lavish vacations. Yet, in this pursuit, we risk losing touch with what truly matters. The thrill of a new

purchase fades; the memory of shared laughter endures. Perhaps it's time to redefine abundance—not as accumulation, but as appreciation.

3. **The Currency of Time**: Every dollar spent is a fragment of time. Think about it: You exchanged hours of work for that latte, that gadget, that impulse buy. Was it worth it? Time is finite; spend it wisely. Invest in experiences that enrich your soul, not just your wardrobe.
4. **The Art of Mindful Spending**: Pause before swiping that card. Ask yourself: Does this align with my values? Will it bring lasting joy? Mindful spending isn't about deprivation; it's about intention. Allocate resources to what truly matters—health, relationships, growth.
5. **The Guilt of Excess**: Overspending breeds guilt. We've all felt it—the pang when the credit card bill arrives, the heaviness of cluttered closets. But guilt isn't a prison; it's a compass. Let it guide you toward conscious choices. Remember, the best things in life aren't things.
6. **The Joy of Simplicity**: Minimalism isn't deprivation; it's liberation. Simplify your life—declutter your space, streamline your expenses. Find joy in less. As Antoine de Saint-Exupéry said, "Perfection is achieved not when there is nothing more to add, but when there is nothing left to take away."
7. **The Legacy of Purpose**: Imagine your legacy—a tapestry woven with threads of impact. What story will it tell? Will it be about possessions amassed or lives touched? Perhaps it's time to shift focus—from "What can I buy?" to "What can I give?"
8. **The Abundance of Gratitude**: Gratitude is the antidote to mindless spending. Pause daily; count blessings. A sunrise, a shared meal, a heartfelt conversation—they're priceless. When you appreciate life's simple gifts, you spend less on fleeting pleasures.
9. **The Freedom of Financial Wellness**: Picture a life unburdened by debt, where choices aren't dictated by bills. It's possible. Budget wisely, save diligently, invest thoughtfully. Financial wellness isn't about restriction; it's about empowerment.
10. **The Symphony of Enough**: "Enough" is a powerful word. It's the sweet spot where contentment meets aspiration. Strive for it. When you focus

on what truly matters, you'll find abundance in simplicity.

In closing, dear readers, may you dance through life with grace—spending not just money, but moments, wisely. May your choices resonate with purpose, and may your legacy be a symphony of enough.

"*Perhaps you've been focusing too much on spending.*" – Unknown

May your financial steps lead you toward fulfillment, not just accumulation.

🌟💰

Lucky Numbers 53, 51, 8, 2, 48, 16

14

Random Act of Kindness

Your random act of kindness today will spread quickly to others.

Ladies and gentlemen, esteemed readers of "Fortune Cookie Coaching," welcome.

I stand before you today to share a powerful message that can change the world. It revolves around a simple yet profound idea: Your random act of kindness today will spread quickly to others.

In a world that often seems consumed by negativity and self-interest, it is easy to forget how much impact a small act of kindness can have. But let me assure you, every act matters. Whether it's lending a hand to someone in need, offering a smile to a stranger, or even just listening to a friend, the ripples created by these acts reverberate far beyond our immediate surroundings.

Imagine yourself as a pebble, dropping into a calm pond. As you penetrate the water's surface, you create a series of concentric circles that extend outward, reaching ever wider with each passing second. Similarly, when you choose to do something kind for someone, that initial action sets off a chain reaction that has the power to touch countless lives.

Kindness is contagious. When we choose to be kind, we inspire and encourage others to follow in our footsteps. By taking the initiative to spread positivity, we create a domino effect that can reshape communities, transform relationships, and foster a sense of unity among us all.

But let us not underestimate the power of even the smallest acts. Sometimes, it is the simplest gestures that carry the greatest weight. Something as seemingly insignificant as holding the door for a stranger, complimenting a coworker, or expressing gratitude to a loved one can create a ripple effect that has the potential to touch hearts and change lives.

So today, I urge each and every one of you to embrace the potential within you. Embrace the power you possess to make a positive difference. No matter who you are or where you come from, your random act of kindness can transcend barriers and bring people together.

Remember, the energy you put into the world is not finite. It multiplies and spreads, touching lives you may never know or even hear about. Your kind words, compassionate deeds, and selfless acts have the extraordinary ability to create a chain reaction of goodness that reverberates throughout society.

Let us be the catalysts for change, the beacons of hope, and the champions of kindness. Together, let us make a commitment to perform one random act of kindness every day. And let us watch in awe as the power of our collective compassion transforms the world around us.

Thank you, and may kindness always be the language we speak.

> *Note: This speech is meant to motivate and inspire, encouraging individuals to embrace kindness and spread positivity. Remember, words alone are not enough; let your actions reflect the spirit of kindness.*

Learn Chinese — 18
十八　shi ba

15

Path to success

YOU ARE ONLY STARTING ON YOUR PATH TO SUCCESS.

Ladies and gentlemen, esteemed readers of "Fortune Cookie Coaching," welcome.

Today, I invite you to embark on an exhilarating journey that will ignite your spirit and unlock the boundless potential within you. It is a journey punctuated by resilience, determination, and an unwavering belief in your ability to conquer any challenge that arises.

As you hold this book in your hands, allow yourself to envision a future filled with boundless possibilities and unimaginable accomplishments. The words on these pages act as a compass, guiding you towards a horizon brimming with purpose, growth, and outstanding achievements.

You see, success is not merely a destination reserved for a chosen few; it is an ongoing pursuit that knows no limitations. It thrives beyond the realms of fame or fortune and instead resides in the moments when you surpass your own limits, embrace discomfort, and seek constant self-improvement.

Consider this: the most magnificent oak tree begins as a minute acorn nestled beneath the soil. With time, nourishment, and an unwavering commitment to growth, it transforms into a towering symbol of strength and resilience. Similarly, you are that acorn, brimming with untapped potential and boundless opportunities.

Your journey to success commences today, right here and now. Have faith in yourself and your abilities, as you possess a unique blend of talents, passions, and dreams that only you can bring to the world. Embrace the challenges that lie ahead, for they serve as stepping stones shaping you into the extraordinary individual destined for greatness.

Along your path, you will undoubtedly encounter setbacks, obstacles, and moments of self-doubt. However, view each setback as an opportunity for growth and every roadblock as a chance to develop unwavering resilience and tap into the depths of your determination. Embrace these moments with vigor and conviction, recognizing that they are the catalysts propelling you towards extraordinary accomplishments.

Success is not a linear trajectory but rather a meandering voyage filled with ups and downs, twists and turns. It is precisely within these twists and turns that you will discover your true strength, unyielding resolve, and unshakeable faith in yourself.

Therefore, my dear reader, as you turn the pages of this book, let it serve as a constant reminder that you are just scratching the surface of your journey to success. Allow these words to inspire and uplift you, igniting a fire within your soul that propels you towards your wildest dreams.

Believe in yourself, for you are more than capable of achieving greatness far beyond your wildest imagination. Embrace each experience, for they are the steppingstones guiding you to extraordinary heights. And above all, always remember that this journey belongs to you and you alone.

You are the captain of your own destiny, the author of your own narrative. With each forward step, you inch closer to becoming the best possible version of yourself. So, let your journey commence with a resounding declaration: "I am at the beginning of an incredible path to success!"

Now, let us embark on this magnificent adventure together, knowing that the possibilities are endless and the rewards immeasurable. Take a bold step forward with unwavering courage, for your path to success awaits.

Wishing you a wealth of inspiration and steadfast determination on your extraordinary journey.

With wholehearted belief in your boundless potential,

9 12 17 18 44 48

Lucky Numbers

16

The usefulness of a cup

The usefulness of a cup is in its emptiness.

L adies and gentlemen, esteemed readers of "Fortune Cookie Coaching," welcome.

Thank you for joining me today as we embark on a journey of self-discovery and empowerment. In a world filled with noise and distractions, it's crucial to pause and reflect on the profound wisdom encapsulated in the simple yet powerful phrase, "The usefulness of a cup is in its emptiness."

Imagine a cup, pristine and waiting to be filled with endless possibilities. Just like that cup, our lives are vessels ready to be filled with experiences, knowledge, and the richness of our dreams. But let's not overlook the essence of emptiness—the space that allows for growth, evolution, and the infusion of new ideas.

In the realm of search engine optimization (SEO), we often emphasize the importance of content. It's true, content is the lifeblood of digital success. However, let's take a moment to consider the parallel with our lives. The emptiness in the cup represents the blank canvas upon which we can paint our stories, dreams, and aspirations. In the digital landscape, it symbolizes the potential for fresh, relevant, and captivating content that not only attracts search engines but resonates with our audience.

Just as a cup is most useful when empty, our minds and hearts are most receptive when open. Embrace the emptiness as an opportunity for learning, innovation, and personal development. In the vast world of SEO, staying current with trends and adapting to algorithm changes is crucial. It's about acknowledging the gaps in our knowledge and filling them with the thirst for improvement.

Consider this: when a cup is filled to the brim, it can no longer accept anything more. Similarly, when our lives are overflowing with the clutter of negativity, self-doubt, or outdated strategies, there is no room for the fresh ideas and perspectives that drive success in the ever-evolving digital landscape.

Let the emptiness of the cup inspire you to constantly seek improvement, to stay agile in the face of change, and to remain open to the vast opportunities that surround us. The usefulness of a cup lies not only in its ability to hold, but in its capacity to release, renew, and embrace the next challenge.

So, let us approach our lives and our digital endeavors with the wisdom of the empty cup. Embrace the space for growth, fill it with purpose, and watch as the richness of your experiences and content spills over, leaving an indelible mark on the world.

May your cup be ever-empty, and your journey abundantly fulfilling.

LEARN CHINESE - To catch a cold
感(gǎn) 冒(mào)
Lucky Numbers 51, 5, 20, 50, 15, 55

17

Politeness cost nothing

Politeness: A Priceless Virtue that Yields Boundless Rewards

Politeness costs nothing and gains everything.

L adies and gentlemen, esteemed readers of "Fortune Cookie Coaching," welcome.

In today's fast-paced world, where interactions can often be cold and detached, the enduring value of politeness should never be underestimated. As the saying goes, "Politeness cost nothing and gains everything." This simple phrase holds great wisdom, reminding us of the power of respectful and considerate behavior.

The Priceless Benefits of Politeness

Politeness, though often overlooked, has the ability to transform our lives and relationships in numerous ways:

1. Building Meaningful Connections

Politeness opens doors and bridges gaps between individuals. By treating others with kindness and respect, we foster an environment of trust and understanding. Genuine connections are formed through polite interactions, enabling us to cultivate lasting relationships.

2. Enhancing Communication

When we communicate with politeness, our messages are delivered with grace and tact. This fosters effective communication, allowing for a smoother exchange of ideas and opinions. Polite conversations create a space where everyone feels heard and valued.

3. Promoting Professionalism

Politeness is an invaluable asset in the professional realm. It cultivates a positive work environment, improves teamwork, and enhances leadership skills. Professionals who exhibit politeness are more likely to be respected and admired by their peers, superiors, and clients.

4. Resolving Conflict Peacefully

In times of disagreement or conflict, politeness serves as a powerful tool for resolution. By approaching difficult situations with grace and respect, we can diffuse tensions and find common ground. Politeness enables us to navigate conflicts constructively, paving the way for peaceful resolutions.

5. Elevating Personal Well-being

The act of being polite uplifts not only those around us but ourselves as well. Politeness fosters empathy, compassion, and gratitude, leading to a more positive mindset and an improved sense of personal well-being. By exhibiting politeness, we contribute to a happier and more harmonious world.

Embrace Politeness and Reap the Rewards

In a society where polite gestures may sometimes be overlooked, it is crucial to remember that being polite costs us nothing, while the benefits are immeasurable. Let us embody politeness as a shining example to those around us, and in doing so, create a world where kindness and respect are cherished values.

7 11 18 21 24 34

Lucky Numbers

18

Simple Kindness

Your simple kindness today will be rewarded multiple times.

L adies and gentlemen, esteemed readers of "Fortune Cookie Coaching," welcome.

Good morning, afternoon, or evening everyone! Today, I want to talk to you about the power of simple kindness and how it can bring about incredible rewards in our lives.

You see, kindness is not just a single act of generosity; it's a ripple effect that touches the lives of others in ways we may never fully comprehend. When you extend a helping hand, lend an ear, or offer a word of encouragement, you are sowing the seeds of positivity and compassion that can change the world around you.

In our fast-paced society, it's easy to get caught up in our own lives and forget the impact we can have on others. But let me tell you, every act of kindness matters, no matter how small it may seem. Whether it's a smile to a stranger, a compliment to a coworker, or a charitable gesture towards someone in need, your actions have the power to make a lasting difference.

But why should you embrace kindness? Because it not only brings joy to those around you but also cultivates a sense of fulfillment within yourself. When you choose to be kind, you elevate your own spirit and create a positive energy that attracts success and happiness.

Now, here's the thing about kindness: it's not about seeking immediate rewards or recognition. It's about genuinely caring for others, without expecting anything in return. However, the beauty of kindness lies in its inherent tendency to come back to us in unexpected ways.

When you sow the seeds of kindness, you're cultivating a garden of goodwill and positive connections. You'll find that people are naturally drawn to your warmth and compassion. Opportunities will arise, doors will open, and new relationships will blossom because of the genuine connections you've nurtured through your simple acts of kindness.

And guess what? The rewards of kindness are not limited to the relationships you forge; they extend to your personal growth and self-improvement as well. When you consistently practice kindness, you cultivate a mindset of empathy, gratitude, and resilience, which are essential qualities for success in both personal and professional endeavors.

So, let me leave you with this thought: Embrace the power of kindness in your life. Make it a habit to spread positivity and compassion wherever you go. Your simple acts of kindness today will not only brighten someone's day but also create a ripple effect of goodness that will come back to you in ways you may not even imagine.

Remember, your simple kindness today will be rewarded multiple times. So, let's go forth and make a difference in the world, one act of kindness at a time.

Thank you.

10 15 16 25 31 32

Lucky Numbers

19

Knowledge and ignorance

☺ The only good is knowledge and the only evil ignorance.☺

Ladies and gentlemen, seekers of wisdom and champions of growth,

Today, I invite you to embark on a journey—a journey fueled by the profound words of ancient wisdom: **"The only good is knowledge, and the only evil is ignorance."**

Let us unravel the layers of this truth together:

1. **Knowledge Illuminates**: Imagine knowledge as a beacon in the darkness. It dispels shadows, revealing pathways to understanding. When you seek knowledge, you ignite a torch that guides you through life's labyrinth. Every book you read, every lesson you learn, every conversation you engage in—these are sparks that light your way.
2. **Ignorance: The Silent Saboteur**: Ignorance isn't merely lack of information; it's a silent saboteur. It thrives in closed minds, stifling growth and perpetuating prejudice. Ignorance blinds us to possibilities, shackles us to outdated beliefs, and fuels fear. It's the root of division, conflict, and missed opportunities.

3. **The Quest for Truth**: Knowledge isn't static; it's a river that flows, carving new channels. Seek truth relentlessly. Question assumptions. Challenge dogmas. As Socrates himself did, engage in the Socratic method—question, probe, and emerge wiser. Remember, true knowledge isn't about knowing everything; it's about knowing how much you don't know.
4. **Empathy and Compassion**: Knowledge breeds empathy. When you understand diverse perspectives, you bridge gaps. Ignorance, on the other hand, erects walls. Choose empathy over judgment. Walk in others' shoes. Seek to understand before being understood. As Maya Angelou said, "Do the best you can until you know better. Then when you know better, do better."
5. **The Power of Curiosity**: Curiosity is the heartbeat of knowledge. It's the childlike wonder that propels us forward. Cultivate it. Ask questions. Explore. Dive into books, travel, and conversations. Curiosity is the antidote to ignorance—it opens doors, dismantles biases, and fuels innovation.
6. **Humility and Epistemic Humility**: Acknowledge your limitations. Epistemic humility—the recognition that our understanding is finite—keeps arrogance at bay. Embrace the vastness of the unknown. Be open to learning from unexpected sources—a child's innocence, an elder's wisdom, or a stranger's story.
7. **Breaking Chains**: Ignorance chains us to outdated paradigms. Break free. Educate yourself on history, science, art, and culture. Read voraciously. Attend lectures. Engage in lifelong learning. Ignorance thrives in echo chambers; knowledge flourishes in open minds.
8. **Be a Torchbearer**: As you acquire knowledge, share it generously. Be a torchbearer for others. Mentor, teach, and uplift. Remember, your light doesn't diminish by lighting another's candle. In the words of Rumi, "The wound is the place where the light enters you."
9. **Choose Enlightenment**: Ignorance breeds fear; knowledge breeds courage. Choose enlightenment over darkness. When faced with a choice, ask, "Does this lead me toward knowledge or deeper into

ignorance?" Opt for the path that expands your mind and enriches your soul.
10. **The Ripple Effect**: Knowledge isn't selfish; it ripples outward. When you learn, you empower others. Share your insights, write your truths, and contribute to collective wisdom. Your legacy isn't measured by possessions; it's etched in minds you've enlightened.

In closing, dear readers, let us embrace knowledge as our compass, our North Star. Let us banish ignorance, not with judgment, but with illumination. For in knowledge lies our liberation, our transformation, and our shared destiny.

"The only good is knowledge, and the only evil is ignorance." – Socrates

May your quest for knowledge be relentless, your heart open, and your impact everlasting. ✨📚

6 16 25 33 35 42

Lucky numbers

20

Do your best

> For he who always does his best,
> his best will better grow.

Esteemed readers of "Fortune Cookie Coaching,"

Today, I stand before you, not merely as a coach but as a fellow traveler on this remarkable journey called life. Our paths intersect here, where wisdom meets aspiration, and where the seeds of greatness are sown.

Let us delve into the profound truth encapsulated in these words: **"For he who always does his best, his best will better grow."**

1. **The Unfolding Journey**: Life is a canvas, and each day is a stroke of the brush. As you commit to doing your best, remember that growth isn't linear—it's an unfolding journey. Your best today becomes the foundation for a better tomorrow. Embrace the process; celebrate progress over perfection.
2. **The Power of Consistency**: Excellence isn't a one-time act; it's a habit. When you consistently give your best—whether in work, relationships, or personal growth—you create a ripple effect. Small efforts compound

into significant results. As Aristotle said, "We are what we repeatedly do."
3. **Stretch Beyond Comfort**: Growth lies beyond comfort zones. Imagine a tree—its roots stretch deep into the earth, anchoring it, while its branches reach for the sky. Similarly, stretch your abilities, learn new skills, and embrace challenges. Mediocrity resides in comfort; greatness thrives in expansion.
4. **Learn, Adapt, Evolve**: Your best today need not be your best forever. Learn from failures, adapt to changing circumstances, and evolve. The caterpillar doesn't resist transformation; it becomes the butterfly. Likewise, let life's winds shape you, not break you.
5. **Celebrate Progress, Not Perfection**: Perfection is an illusion; progress is real. Acknowledge your efforts, even when outcomes fall short. Each step forward—no matter how small—is a victory. As Confucius wisely said, "It does not matter how slowly you go as long as you do not stop."
6. **The Art of Mastery**: Mastery isn't about reaching a finish line; it's about falling in love with the process. Whether you're mastering a skill, nurturing relationships, or sculpting your character, immerse yourself. The potter molds clay, not in haste, but with intention.
7. **Plant Seeds of Excellence**: Your best isn't just for you; it's a gift to others. Plant seeds of excellence wherever you go. Be the mentor who inspires, the friend who listens, and the colleague who uplifts. Your legacy isn't in titles; it's in hearts touched.
8. **Embrace Failure as Feedback**: When you stumble, don't berate yourself; learn. Failure isn't fatal; it's feedback. Thomas Edison didn't see his thousand attempts at the light bulb as failures; he saw them as steps toward success. Embrace setbacks—they're stepping stones.
9. **The Joy of Mastery**: Mastery isn't a burden; it's a privilege. Whether you're a pianist, a chef, or a parent, relish the journey. The sculptor doesn't rush; each chisel stroke shapes the masterpiece. Your best today contributes to the symphony of your life.
10. **The Ripple Effect**: Your commitment to excellence influences others. When they witness your dedication, they're inspired to raise their own

standards. Be the candle that ignites other flames. As Maya Angelou beautifully said, "When you know better, do better."

In closing, dear readers, may you embrace the paradox: Your best is both a destination and a perpetual sunrise. As you strive, remember that growth isn't a sprint; it's a dance with eternity.

"For he who always does his best, his best will better grow." – Unknown

May your best today be the catalyst for a brighter, bolder tomorrow.

有知識就是好，無知識就是不好。

21

Some fortune cookies

Some fortune cookies contain no fortune.

Some Fortune Cookies Contain No Fortune: Embrace the Power of Creating Your Own Destiny

Ladies and gentlemen, esteemed readers of "Fortune Cookie Coaching," welcome.

What if I told you that sometimes fortune cookies contain no fortune? It may sound disappointing at first, but it actually holds a profound message within. Life is not always about waiting for fate or external circumstances to determine your path. It's about taking control of your own destiny and creating your own fortune.

In this world of uncertainties and unpredictability, it's easy to feel lost or at the mercy of external forces. We may stumble upon fortune cookies that lack a piece of wisdom or a prophecy. But instead of feeling discouraged, let it serve as a reminder that your fate is not destined solely by chance.

True empowerment lies in embracing the power of creating your own destiny. It's about taking charge of your life, setting your own goals, and pursuing them with unwavering determination. Remember, fortune favors the bold, and those who believe in their own abilities to shape their future.

It's time to break free from the confines of passivity and embrace a proactive mindset. Start by focusing on personal growth and self-improvement. Cultivate a success mindset that thrives on positivity and resilience. Surround yourself with inspirational coaching and motivational speeches to fuel your inner fire.

Fortune cookies may come and go, but the message remains clear: the power to transform lies within you. Seize the opportunity to consciously shape your path, to navigate through challenges, and to embrace every setback as a stepping stone towards personal development.

Remember, success is not defined solely by external accolades or monetary gains. It's about finding fulfillment and purpose in your journey. Set meaningful goals, both big and small, and work towards them with relentless dedication. Celebrate every milestone along the way, for it is these moments that truly shape your character and strengthen your resolve.

So the next time you crack open a fortune cookie and find it devoid of a fortune, smile and recognize the hidden opportunity it presents. Embrace the freedom to create your own destiny, guided by your dreams, aspirations, and unwavering determination.

Fortune may come in various forms, but the greatest fortune of all is the power you hold within to shape your own future. Believe in yourself, take decisive action, and let your unyielding spirit be the driving force behind your success.

4 9 19 22 32 45

Lucky Numbers

22

No need to worry!

*No need to worry!
You will always have
everything that you need.*

Ladies and gentlemen, esteemed readers of "Fortune Cookie Coaching," welcome.

No need to worry! You will always have everything that you need.

Greetings, dear friends and fellow seekers of motivation and inspiration! Today, I stand before you with a resounding message: no need to worry! You will always have everything that you need.

Life, with its twists and turns, can often leave us feeling overwhelmed and uncertain. It is during these moments of doubt that we tend to question if we have what it takes to overcome the challenges that lie ahead. But fear not, for today, I am here to remind you of the unwavering truth that resides within each and every one of us.

Believe me when I say that you possess immense strength and resilience, capable of weathering any storm that comes your way. The universe has a unique way of providing exactly what we need, precisely when we need it.

Each obstacle that appears before you is an opportunity in disguise, leading you closer to your destined path.

In times of uncertainty, remember this: the seeds of greatness reside within your soul. Nurture them with determination, water them with persistence, and watch as they flourish into remarkable achievements. Let go of doubt and embrace the infinite possibilities that await you.

It is essential to foster a positive mindset and align your thoughts towards abundance and gratitude. When you emit vibrations of positivity and gratitude into the world, the universe conspires to bring forth all that your heart desires. Trust in the process, have faith in yourself, and vibrant blessings will manifest in unimaginable ways.

No need to worry about the challenges that lie ahead, for you are equipped with everything you need to conquer them. You possess an innate resilience that knows no bounds and a wellspring of creativity that can reshape your reality. Believe in the power within you, and watch as you transform obstacles into stepping stones towards success.

Remember, dear friends, that the journey towards personal growth and self-improvement is not a solitary one. Surround yourself with a supportive community and seek guidance from mentors who uplift and inspire you. Together, we can conquer any adversity and achieve greatness beyond imagination.

So, my dear friends, let this message resonate within your soul: no need to worry! You will always have everything that you need. Embrace the challenges, nurture your dreams, and let your light shine brightly, igniting the path for others to follow.

Believe in yourself, trust the journey, and watch as the universe conspires to make all your dreams come true. Your time is now, and greatness awaits you. Go forth with confidence, knowing that you are destined for greatness.

NO NEED TO WORRY!

LEARN CHINESE - Chicken

鸡(jī) 肉 (ròu)

Lucky Numbers 7, 53, 15, 16, 38, 47

23

Desert sands

You will soon be crossing desert sands for a fun vacation.

Embrace the Journey: Crossing Desert Sands for a Fun Vacation
    Ladies and gentlemen, esteemed readers of "Fortune Cookie Coaching," welcome.

I stand before you today with an invigorating message of hope, resilience, and the power of adventure. With every step you take, with each hurdle you conquer, you move closer to experiencing the ultimate reward of a fun-filled vacation. So, let's dive into the depths of our imagination and envision a remarkable journey across the vast desert sands.

Picture this: You're standing at the edge of an endless expanse of golden sand dunes, stretching as far as the eye can see. The scorching sun casts its warm, welcoming rays upon your face. In this moment, you realize that you are about to embark on a remarkable adventure, one that will leave an indelible mark on your soul.

The desert may appear unforgiving and daunting at first glance, but within its vastness lies the promise of discovery and transformation. As the grains of sand shift beneath your feet, so will your perceptions and limitations. You will find strength you never knew existed within you.

With each step forward, you will encounter obstacles. The blistering heat may try to sap your energy, mirages may attempt to deceive your senses, and doubt may creep into your mind. But remember this: the greatest achievements in life are often born out of adversity.

As you navigate the wilderness of the desert, you will uncover hidden treasures along the way. From witnessing the breathtaking beauty of a majestic sunset painting the sky in hues of purple and orange, to feeling the exhilaration of conquering the tallest dunes, the desert rewards those who dare to venture forth.

The journey itself is a testament to your spirit, determination, and unwavering belief in the power of exploration. It is not merely about reaching your destination, but about embracing the challenges that come your way. It is about finding joy and growth in the face of uncertainty.

And remember, dear friends, that your adventure does not end with the final step taken on the sandy shores. It is the memories you create, the lessons you learn, and the transformative experience you undergo that will stay with you forever.

So, let's gather our courage, pack our bags, and set forth on this incredible journey. We have the opportunity to cross the desert sands, not just for a vacation, but for a life-changing adventure filled with laughter, growth, and profound moments of self-discovery.

In the words of Ralph Waldo Emerson, "Do not go where the path may lead, go instead where there is no path and leave a trail." Embrace the unknown, for it is through the challenges that lie ahead that we truly find ourselves and create the most memorable moments of our lives.

May your path be filled with resilience, courage, and an unwavering spirit of adventure. Believe in your ability to conquer the desert sands, and soon enough, you will revel in the joy of a fun-filled vacation that will forever be etched in your heart.

Thank you.

Learn Chinese — Chinese
中国的／汉语　*zhong guo de/han yu*

24

Get things done

> Your energy returns and you get things done.

Ladies and gentlemen, esteemed readers of "Fortune Cookie Coaching," welcome.

I stand before you today with a simple yet powerful message: "Your energy returns and you get things done." These words carry a profound truth that resonates with each one of us on our journey towards success. Today, I want to inspire you to harness the power within you, unleash your potential, and propel yourself towards achieving your goals.

In a world filled with challenges and uncertainties, it's easy to feel overwhelmed and drained of energy. Life's demands can often take a toll on our motivation and enthusiasm. But, my friends, it's crucial to remember that within you lies an incredible reservoir of energy waiting to be tapped into.

Imagine a life where you wake up every morning with a renewed sense of purpose and vigor. Picture yourself facing challenges head-on, fueled by a boundless well of determination. This isn't a distant dream; it's a reality waiting for you to embrace. When you tap into your inner energy, remarkable things start to happen.

The key is to identify the sources that recharge your spirit and surround yourself with positivity. Whether it's engaging in activities you love, spending time with supportive friends and family, or pursuing your passions, these are the building blocks of a fulfilling and energized life. As you align your actions with your values, you'll find that your energy not only returns but intensifies, becoming an unstoppable force propelling you forward.

Now, let's talk about getting things done. We live in an era where productivity is highly valued, and achieving our goals requires focused effort. The beauty of regaining your energy is that it fuels your productivity engine. You become more resilient, creative, and efficient in tackling the tasks at hand. Procrastination takes a back seat as you embrace a can-do attitude, pushing through obstacles with unwavering determination.

But how do you kickstart this transformative process? It begins with a mindset shift. Believe in your abilities, acknowledge your strengths, and visualize success. Set clear, achievable goals and break them down into manageable steps. Celebrate small victories along the way, for they are the stepping stones to monumental achievements.

In the realm of search engine optimization (SEO), the principles are analogous. Your website's visibility and success hinge on the energy you invest in optimizing it for search engines. The more you refine your content, enhance user experience, and stay attuned to SEO trends, the higher your digital presence will soar.

So, my friends, as you embark on this journey of renewed energy and heightened productivity, remember that the power to shape your destiny lies within you. Your energy returns, and you get things done. Embrace this mantra, apply it to every aspect of your life, and watch as the universe aligns to support your endeavors.

Together, let's energize our ambitions, conquer challenges, and revel in the satisfaction of getting things done. The world is waiting for the brilliance that only you can bring. Go out there, ignite your energy, and make your mark!

Thank you.

2 23 32 45 48 49

Lucky Numbers

25

Necessity

Necessity does everything well.

Ladies and gentlemen, esteemed readers of "Fortune Cookie Coaching," welcome.
    Today, I stand before you to share a powerful truth - "Necessity does everything well." These words hold a profound meaning that can guide us through the myriad challenges of life. In moments of uncertainty, when we face overwhelming obstacles, it is this very necessity that ignites the fire within us and propels us forward.

Necessity has been the driving force behind countless achievements in human history. It has sparked innovation, resilience, and unwavering determination. When the odds seemed insurmountable, individuals and societies have risen above their circumstances and triumphed because they embraced the power of necessity.

Embracing necessity involves recognizing the inherent potential within ourselves. It requires us to tap into our deepest reservoirs of strength, understanding that we possess the ability to overcome any obstacle that stands in our way. Necessity empowers us to discover the hidden capabilities and talents that reside within us, waiting to be unleashed.

Necessity teaches us to adapt and evolve. It pushes us beyond our comfort zones, urging us to challenge the status quo and seek new paths to success. When faced with the choice of either succumbing to adversity or rising above it, necessity compels us to choose the latter, pushing us to develop the qualities of resilience, determination, and perseverance.

Every great achievement in human history has been driven by the necessity to improve and grow. From scientific breakthroughs to artistic masterpieces, from monumental societal changes to personal transformations - all have been fueled by the belief that necessity does everything well. It is this conviction that has propelled individuals to reach beyond their limits and soar to great heights.

So, my friends, let us embrace necessity as our guiding light. Let us revel in the challenges we encounter, for they serve as catalysts for our own growth and development. Let us remember that it is in our moments of necessity that we discover our true potential and manifest our dreams into reality.

As we navigate the journey of life, let us never forget the power of necessity. May it inspire us, drive us, and enable us to overcome every obstacle that comes our way. Remember, necessity does everything well, and it is within each of us to harness its immense power and forge our own paths to success.

Thank you.

有知識就是好，無知識就是不好。

26

Understanding

> *The beginning of all understanding is innocent.*

The Beginning of All Understanding is Innocent

Ladies and gentlemen, esteemed readers of "Fortune Cookie Coaching," fellow seekers of personal growth and enlightenment welcome.

I stand before you today to share a profound truth—a truth that holds the power to mold our perception, shape our actions, and ignite the flames of success within each of us. It is my firm belief that the beginning of all understanding is innocent.

In this ever-evolving world, filled with complexities and challenges, it is easy to lose sight of the simplicity that underlies wisdom. We often find ourselves entangled in the webs of doubt and uncertainty, searching relentlessly for answers. But what if I told you that the key to unlocking the gates of understanding lies in embracing our innate innocence?

When we embark on a journey of self-discovery, we realize that in our purest form, we possess an unadulterated curiosity—a thirst for knowledge and a desire to explore the uncharted realms of our potential. It is during our initial stages of learning that we lay the groundwork for a lifetime of insight and growth. Just as a seed requires a nurturing environment to sprout, our minds require a fertile foundation of curiosity and innocence to blossom into all-encompassing understanding.

Innocence allows us to question without fear, to embrace the unknown without hesitation, and to perceive the world with fresh eyes. It opens doors to infinite possibilities and empowers us to uncover the deepest truths that lie hidden beneath the surface.

Think back to a time when the world was a landscape of endless wonders, where each experience was a lesson in itself, and each challenge was an opportunity for growth. It was during those moments of innocence that we discovered the power of resilience, determination, and unwavering belief in ourselves. We dared to dream boldly, stepping outside our comfort zones and delving into unexplored territories.

Today, I urge you to reconnect with that inner child—the embodiment of innocence within us all. Embrace the pure curiosity and unwavering optimism that once fueled your every endeavor. Let go of the shackles of doubt and refocus your gaze on the boundless realm of possibilities.

Remember, success is not measured solely by the accolades we accumulate, but by the growth we experience along the way. By embracing our inherent innocence, we invite understanding and enlightenment into every aspect of our lives. This radiant light of understanding has the power to illuminate our path, guiding us towards our goals and aspirations.

As we tread the path of self-improvement and personal growth, let us never forget that the beginning of all understanding is innocent. Nurture that innocence, let it be the guiding force that propels you towards greatness. Believe in yourself, dare to dream, and let understanding unfold in ways you could never have imagined.

Thank you.

10 28 30 33 41 44

Lucky Numbers

27

Desire is explosive

> *Desire, like the atom, is explosive with creative force.*

D*esire: The Explosive Creative Force*
Ladies and gentlemen, esteemed readers of "Fortune Cookie Coaching," welcome.

Today, I stand before you to ignite the flame of desire within your hearts. For desire, like the atom, holds immense power—a power that can reshape your reality and transform your dreams into a tangible existence.

Desire is not a mere whim or fleeting thought; it is the driving force that propels us forward and fuels our aspirations. It is the spark that ignites our inner fire, compelling us to reach new heights and accomplish the extraordinary.

Just like the atom, desire possesses an explosive capacity for creation. It has the potential to break through barriers, overcome challenges, and shatter existing limitations. It is through desire that great inventions have been born, artistic masterpieces have been painted, and groundbreaking discoveries have been made.

Let me assure you, dear friends, that your desires are not to be taken lightly. They are the whispers of your soul, guiding you towards your true purpose and greatest potential. Embrace these desires with open arms, for they are the roadmap to your destiny.

However, it is not enough to simply harbor desires within the depths of your being. You must unleash them with conviction, intention, and unwavering belief. Give your desires wings to soar, and watch as they manifest into reality.

In the pursuit of your desires, obstacles may arise, doubts may cloud your mind, and fear may attempt to hold you back. But remember this: just as the atom overcomes the forces that bind it, you too possess the resilience and strength to overcome any adversity that crosses your path.

Nurture your desires, cultivate them with unwavering determination, and infuse them with relentless action. Feed the flames of your aspirations, for they are the very essence of your existence. With each step forward, inch closer to the life you envision, let your desires guide you towards greatness.

So, dear friends, I implore you to embrace the explosive creative force that resides within you. Awaken the power of desire, channel its energy, and unleash it upon the world. Let your dreams take flight, propelled by the incredible force that desire possesses. And remember, as you move forward towards your ambitions, the universe aligns itself to support your every endeavor.

Thank you.

LEARN CHINESE - Summer

夏(xià)天(tiān)

Lucky Numbers 31, 14, 54, 19, 5, 22

28

Vacation

A much needed vacation will allow you to unwind.

A Much-Needed Vacation: Unwind and Fuel Your Motivation

Ladies and gentlemen, esteemed readers of "Fortune Cookie Coaching," welcome.

I stand before you today to emphasize the importance of taking a much-needed vacation. In a fast-paced world where we are constantly connected and bombarded with responsibilities, it is crucial to recognize the significance of stepping away from the daily grind and embracing the opportunity to unwind.

Picture this: you find yourself amid pristine beaches, surrounded by the serene sound of crashing waves, or exploring new and breathtaking landscapes. A vacation offers a reprieve from the monotony of everyday life, allowing you to rejuvenate your body, mind, and spirit.

But it isn't just about indulging in leisurely activities. A vacation can play a pivotal role in rekindling your motivation. It provides a golden chance to detach yourself from the stressors of work and life, allowing you to regain clarity and perspective. By temporarily distancing yourself from routine obligations, you create the mental space necessary for fresh ideas and insights to flourish.

Think about it: when was the last time you took a step back, unburdened yourself, and truly focused on your own well-being? With the demands of modern society, we often forget to prioritize our mental and emotional health. Yet, it is in these moments of respite that we find the strength and inspiration to overcome challenges and fuel personal growth.

While basking in the joys and beauty of a well-deserved vacation, you'll rediscover the meaning of self-care and introspection. A retreat from the daily grind will grant you the opportunity to reflect on your priorities, reassess your goals, and pinpoint the areas in your life that require adjustments or improvements.

A vacation is not just a luxury; it is an investment in your own personal development. By carving out time for relaxation and self-reflection, you will find that you return with renewed vigor, a clearer vision, and a mindset ready to navigate the relentless pursuit of success.

As I conclude, let me remind you that you hold within you the power to redefine your journey. Embrace the chance to embark on a well-deserved vacation, as it serves not only as a means of unwinding but as a catalyst for personal and professional growth.

So, my friends, I implore you to prioritize your well-being and consider taking that much-needed vacation. Unwind, explore, rejuvenate, and return fortified with a renewed zest for life!

Thank you.

9 12 17 18 44 48

Lucky Numbers

29

Family reunion

> *A family reunion in the coming months will be a tremendous success!*

A **Family Reunion: A Tremendous Success!**
Ladies and gentlemen, esteemed readers of "Fortune Cookie Coaching," welcome.

I am delighted to stand before you today and share a heartfelt message that will inspire and motivate each and every one of us. As we gather here, filled with anticipation and joy, I want to proclaim with unwavering certainty that our upcoming family reunion in the coming months will be a tremendous success!

This cherished event represents far more than just a gathering of relatives. It symbolizes the strength of our bonds, the richness of our shared experiences, and the love that unites us all. It is an occasion to celebrate our heritage, reflect on the memories we hold dear, and create new moments that will be treasured forever.

In this ever-changing world, where time seems to slip through our fingers like grains of sand, a family reunion serves as an oasis of love and togetherness. It reminds us of the significance of family, serving as a constant reminder that we are part of something greater than ourselves. Our roots run deep, and it is through these connections that we draw strength, support, and guidance.

As we prepare ourselves for this momentous occasion, let us embrace the power of positivity and envision the success that awaits us. A successful family reunion is not solely measured by the number of attendees, the magnificence of the venue, or the eloquence of the speeches. Its true essence lies in the smiles shared, the laughter echoed, and the memories created.

Each one of us has a role to play in making this event an unforgettable experience. Let us come together with open hearts, open minds, and a desire to reconnect, reconnect not only with our immediate family but also with distant relatives whom we have not seen in years. Let us bridge the gaps that time and distance have created, and forge stronger bonds that will stand the test of time.

It is through unity and mutual respect that we shall overcome any obstacles that come our way. Challenges may arise, logistical hurdles may test our patience, but it is our determination and resilience that will ensure the success of this gathering. Believe in the power of our shared love, and together we shall prevail.

In the months leading up to our family reunion, let us keep the flame of excitement burning brightly. Share stories, reminisce about the good times, and express your eagerness to reconnect with loved ones. Spread the word and let's make this reunion a momentous occasion that will be etched in our hearts forever.

So, dear family, as we embark on this journey to celebrate our shared history and create new memories, let us embrace the belief that our family reunion in the coming months will indeed be a tremendous success! With love as our compass and unity as our strength, we will create an atmosphere of joy, laughter, and lifelong connections.

Together, let us make this reunion a shining testament to the power of family and the beauty of unconditional love. May we leave no stone unturned in our efforts, and may the memories we create on this special occasion be cherished for generations to come.

Thank you, and let the countdown to our phenomenal family reunion begin!

With love and excitement,

LEARN CHINESE - To cough

咳(ké)嗽(sòu)

Lucky Numbers 50, 8, 30, 6, 40, 37

30

The daily grind

Don't get so caught up in the daily grind that you never find any time to enjoy yourself.

Don't Get Caught in the Daily Grind—Embrace Life and Find Your Bliss!

Ladies and gentlemen, esteemed readers of "Fortune Cookie Coaching," welcome.

I stand before you today to deliver a motivational speech that will redefine your perspective on life. In a world consumed by the relentless demands of the daily grind, it is crucial to remember the importance of finding time to enjoy ourselves. As we embark on this journey of self-discovery, let us cast aside the shackles of monotony and embrace the beauty that life has to offer.

Embracing the Daily Grind

The daily grind—the repetitive cycle of work and responsibilities—can be all-consuming. We find ourselves entangled in a web of deadlines, tasks, and obligations, often forgetting to take a moment to breathe and appreciate the world around us. However, my friends, it is within our power to break free from this grind and reclaim our right to a fulfilling existence.

Seeking Balance

Yes, we must work diligently to achieve our goals, pursue our passions, and support ourselves and our loved ones. But remember, life is not solely about accomplishment; it is also about savoring the sweet moments that bring us joy. When we neglect to allocate time for ourselves, we miss out on the enchanting experiences that make life truly magnificent.

Embracing Life's Pleasures

Each of us has unique interests and passions that encourage our personal growth and happiness. Whether it's spending quality time with loved ones, engaging in hobbies, exploring new places, or immersing ourselves in art and culture, these moments of bliss are vital for our well-being.

The Consequences of Neglect

By neglecting our need for personal enjoyment, we risk becoming mere cogs in the machinery of life. We end up sailing through existence without truly experiencing the beauty that surrounds us. Let us not allow ourselves to be defined solely by our professional accomplishments, but by the moments of fulfillment and joy that make life worth living.

THE DAILY GRIND

Carving Out Time for Happiness

It is imperative to consciously carve out time for ourselves, for joy, and for personal growth. Resist the allure of endless work, for a life bereft of enjoyment is no life at all. Prioritize self-care, leisure, and pursuing your passions. Block out time in your busy schedule to relish in the simple pleasures that sprinkle happiness into our lives.

In conclusion, my friends, I implore you to break free from the shackles of the daily grind. Remember your worth beyond the tasks and responsibilities that consume your days. Don't get so caught up in the whirlwind of life that you never find any time to enjoy yourself. Seek balance, embrace life's pleasures, and remember that true fulfillment lies not just in accomplishment but in savoring the precious moments that define our existence.

Today, I beseech you to reclaim your right to happiness, to create a life that balances work and play, and to never let the monotony of the daily grind dampen your spirit. May you find the courage to embrace life's adventures, celebrate your achievements, and cherish the time you spend, not only in pursuit of success but in savoring the essence of who you are.

2 18 23 34 38 45

Lucky Numbers

31

The calling

The calling that has sounded will not be the lasting call.

The Calling That Has Sounded Will Not Be the Lasting Call

Ladies and gentlemen, esteemed readers of "Fortune Cookie Coaching," welcome.

Today, I stand before you to remind you of a fundamental truth: the calling that has sounded will not be the lasting call. Life is a journey filled with twists and turns, ups and downs. It is easy to get caught up in the present moment, thinking that the challenges we face are insurmountable. But I am here to tell you that it is not the end.

The path to success is not a straightforward one. It is often riddled with setbacks and obstacles that test our determination and resilience. But it is during these moments of adversity that our true character is revealed. We must remember that every challenge we encounter is an opportunity for growth and personal development.

It is easy to become fixated on one particular calling, one specific goal, and believe that it defines our entire journey. But life has a way of surprising us, of taking us on unexpected detours that lead to even greater possibilities. The calling that has sounded may not be the ultimate destination; it may be merely a stepping stone to something far greater.

In our pursuit of personal and professional growth, it is essential to embrace change and adapt to new opportunities. We must remain open-minded and flexible, willing to explore different paths and expand our horizons. Just because we have heard one call does not mean it will be the lasting one. There is always room for growth, for reevaluation, and for finding new passions and purposes.

So, my friends, I encourage you to never lose hope. When faced with challenges and setbacks, remember that they are not the end of the road but a necessary part of the journey. Embrace the lessons they bring, for they will shape you into a stronger, more resilient individual.

Believe in your abilities and trust that the universe has a plan for you. Keep pushing forward, even when the path seems uncertain. Stay committed to your personal growth and development, knowing that the calling that has sounded will not be the lasting call.

Together, let us embark on this journey with open hearts and determined minds. Let us embrace change, seize new opportunities, and discover the true extent of our potential. The road may be long and challenging, but with resilience, determination, and an unwavering belief in ourselves, we can achieve greatness.

Thank you, and may your journey be filled with purpose, growth, and lasting fulfillment.

Learn Chinese — 18

十八   shi ba

32

Solutions

You will find your solution where you least expect it.

Esteemed readers of "Fortune Cookie Coaching,"

Today, I invite you to embark on a treasure hunt—a quest for solutions that lie hidden in the folds of unexpected moments. The universe whispers: **"You will find your solution where you least expect it."**

1. **The Map of Curiosity**: Imagine life as a vast map, dotted with uncharted territories. Your solution—the X that marks the spot—may not be on the well-trodden paths. It might hide in the margins, behind question marks. Be curious; explore the edges.
2. **The Puzzle Pieces**: Solutions aren't monolithic; they're mosaic. Each piece—a conversation, a daydream, a random encounter—holds a clue. Collect them. Soon, you'll see the bigger picture. Trust that every fragment matters.
3. **The Whisper of Intuition**: Intuition isn't loud; it's a whisper. When you

least expect it, your inner compass nudges. Listen. That hunch—the one you dismiss as coincidence—might be your solution knocking.
4. **The Backroads of Creativity**: Creativity thrives where roads diverge. Take detours. Wander into side streets, explore dead ends. Solutions love to play hide-and-seek in forgotten alleys. Chase them; they giggle.
5. **The Serendipity Café**: Picture a café where serendipity serves coffee. Tomorrow, visit. Sit by the window, sip warmth, and watch. The person at the next table—the one reading your favorite book—might hold your solution. Strike up a conversation; the universe loves dialogue.
6. **The Quantum Leap**: Not all solutions are linear; some are quantum leaps—the ones that defy logic. They're disguised as risks, but they're really portals. When you leap, you don't just cross; you transform. Trust the leap; the universe catches you.
7. **The Silence of Stillness**: Solutions aren't always noisy; they thrive in stillness. Meditate, breathe, pause. In the quietude, ideas bloom. Your solution—the seed—awaits germination.
8. **The Unexpected Mentor**: Solutions wear disguises. Sometimes, they arrive as mentors—the stranger on the train, the child with curious eyes. Listen. Their words—the ones you least expect—might hold your breakthrough.
9. **The Dance of Resilience**: Solutions aren't handed out; they're earned. Dance with setbacks, tango with challenges. Each stumble—each bruised knee—shapes your solution. Persevere; the universe admires your resilience.
10. **The Final Revelation**: As we conclude, remember: Solutions aren't elusive; they're playful. They peek from behind clouds, whisper through raindrops. Keep your eyes wide, your heart open. You'll find your solution where you least expect it.

"You will find your solution where you least expect it." – Unknown
May your treasure hunt be fruitful, your surprises delightful, and your solutions abundant. ✨🌿🌏

2 18 23 34 38 45

Lucky numbers

33

Strength

FRIENDS ADMIRE YOUR STRENGTH.

Fortune Cookie Fam, assemble! Today's message isn't just a compliment, it's a recognition of your inner power: **"Friends admire your strength."** And guess what? It's not just your friends who see it. Fortune Cookie Coaching celebrates your strength too!

Sure, strength comes in many forms. It's not all about biceps and bravado. Sometimes, true strength lies in:

- **Resilience:** The ability to bounce back from setbacks and keep moving forward.
- **Compassion:** The courage to be kind, even when it's difficult.
- **Vulnerability:** The strength to share your true self with the world.
- **Perseverance:** The unwavering determination to see things through, even when the going gets tough.
- **Integrity:** The unwavering commitment to your values, no matter the pressure.

These are all forms of strength that your friends admire.

Here's how you can continue cultivating your inner strength:

- **Challenge yourself:** Step outside your comfort zone, face your fears, and push yourself to grow.
- **Practice self-care:** Prioritize your physical and mental well-being to build a foundation of resilience.
- **Embrace vulnerability:** Share your struggles, connect with others, and learn from shared experiences.
- **Celebrate your wins (big and small):** Recognizing your progress fuels your strength and inspires others.
- **Learn from setbacks:** Don't let challenges define you. Analyze what went wrong, pick yourself up, and keep moving forward.

Remember, Fortune Cookie Coaching is your guide on this journey of self-discovery. This book equips you with tools to build confidence, navigate challenges, and cultivate unwavering resilience.

Your strength is an inspiration to those around you. It empowers others to face their own challenges and creates a ripple effect of positive energy. So, Fortune Cookie Fam, go forth and **shine your inner strength on the world!** Be a beacon of resilience, compassion, and integrity. Inspire others, and together, create a more positive and empowered community. Remember, true strength is found within, and you've got it in abundance!

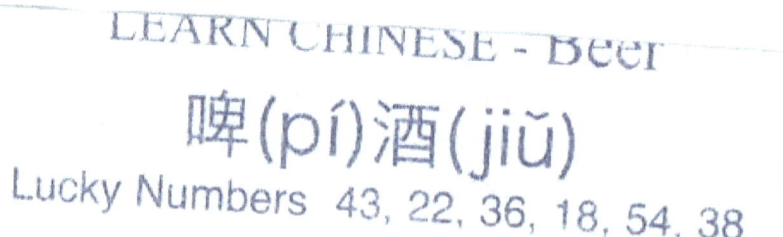

LEARN CHINESE - Beer
啤(pí)酒(jiǔ)
Lucky Numbers 43, 22, 36, 18, 54, 38

34

Improve finances

You will soon have the opportunity to improve your finances.

Esteemed readers of "Fortune Cookie Coaching,"

Today, let us gather around the hearth of possibility, where the flames of opportunity dance. The universe whispers: **"You will soon have the opportunity to improve your finances."**

1. **The Currency of Choice**: Imagine life as a marketplace. Your choices—the coins and bills you exchange—determine your financial destiny. Soon, a new opportunity will knock. Will you invest in knowledge, in relationships, or in your dreams? Choose wisely; the universe accepts no refunds.
2. **The Ledger of Learning**: Every experience is a ledger entry. Some transactions yield profits; others, losses. Soon, you'll encounter a seminar, a mentor, or a book—the ledger will balance. Learn voraciously; knowledge compounds like interest.
3. **The Stock Exchange of Skills**: Your skills are stocks. Some appreciate;

others depreciate. Soon, you'll attend a workshop, acquire a certification, or master a craft—the market will respond. Invest in skills; they pay dividends for life.

4. **The Bank of Boldness**: Courage is your currency. Soon, you'll face a risk—a business venture, a career change, or a leap of faith. Deposit courage; it appreciates over time. The universe rewards audacity.
5. **The Interest of Intention**: Intentions are interest-bearing accounts. Soon, you'll set a goal—a savings target, a debt payoff, or a retirement plan. Compound your intentions; they yield exponential returns.
6. **The Fortune Cookie Portfolio**: Picture a portfolio—a mix of stocks, bonds, and dreams. Soon, you'll diversify—an investment property, a side hustle, or a passion project. Balance risk with reward; the universe allocates accordingly.
7. **The Wealth of Well-Being**: Prosperity isn't just about money; it's about well-being. Soon, you'll prioritize health—a morning jog, a meditation practice, or a good night's sleep. Invest in vitality; it's the foundation of wealth.
8. **The Tax of Time**: Time is your tax collector. Soon, you'll allocate hours—an extra job, a hobby, or volunteering. Spend wisely; time is finite. The universe audits your days.
9. **The Legacy of Generosity**: Wealth isn't hoarded; it's shared. Soon, you'll have surplus—an unexpected bonus, a windfall, or a promotion. Give generously; the universe replenishes open hands.
10. **The Final Dividend**: As we conclude, remember: Opportunities are like shooting stars—they streak across the sky, leaving trails of possibility. Soon, one will blaze your path. Be ready; the universe rewards readiness.

"You will soon have the opportunity to improve your finances." – Unknown

May your financial garden bloom, your investments thrive, and your wealth ripple outward. 🌟💰

IMPROVE FINANCES

8 12 18 32 42 47

Lucky numbers

35

Smiling

 Smiling will take away all your worries.
6 10 13 19 29 34

Ladies and gentlemen, esteemed readers of "Fortune Cookie Coaching," welcome.

I stand before you today with a simple yet profound message: "Smiling will take away all your worries." In a world filled with challenges and uncertainties, it's easy to become overwhelmed by the burdens we carry on our shoulders. But let me assure you that a smile, a genuine and heartfelt expression of joy, has the power to transform our perspective and lighten the heaviest of loads.

Picture this: a world where every frown is replaced with a smile, where optimism triumphs over adversity. It may sound like a utopian dream, but the truth is, the power to make this vision a reality lies within each and every one of us. The act of smiling is not merely a reflex; it is a conscious decision to embrace positivity, resilience, and hope.

Now, you might be wondering, how can a simple smile make such a significant difference? Allow me to share the profound impact that a smile can have on our lives.

Firstly, smiling is contagious. When you share a smile with someone, you create a ripple effect of positivity. Your joy becomes a source of inspiration for others, uplifting their spirits and encouraging a chain reaction of happiness. Imagine the collective strength we can harness when we choose to spread smiles instead of dwelling on our worries.

Secondly, smiling is a natural stress reliever. In the midst of life's challenges, a smile can act as a therapeutic balm, soothing our minds and calming our anxieties. It releases endorphins, the body's natural feel-good chemicals, creating a sense of well-being that transcends the challenges we face.

Furthermore, a smile is a symbol of resilience. It is a declaration that no matter how tough the journey may be, we have the inner strength to face it with grace and optimism. In the face of adversity, a smile becomes a powerful weapon, reminding us that we are capable of overcoming any obstacle that stands in our way.

Now, let's talk about the SEO optimized aspect of our message. In a digital age where information is at our fingertips, it's essential to leverage the power of words to reach a broader audience. By emphasizing the phrase "Smiling will take away all your worries," we not only convey a compelling message but also optimize our content for search engines, making it more accessible to those seeking motivation and inspiration.

In conclusion, my friends, let us embrace the transformative power of a smile. Together, we can create a world where worries dissipate in the radiant glow of positivity. So, wear your smiles proudly, share them generously, and let us build a future where the simple act of smiling becomes the beacon that guides us through life's journey.

Thank you, and may your days be filled with countless reasons to smile.

3 6 10 22 30 41

Lucky Numbers

36

Wondrous opportunity

Be prepared to accept a wondrous opportunity in the days ahead!

Ladies and gentlemen, esteemed readers of "Fortune Cookie Coaching," welcome.

I stand before you today with a message that transcends mere words; it resonates with the rhythm of possibility and the melody of potential. In the grand symphony of life, each note is a chance, and every pause is an opportunity waiting to be seized. Today, I implore you to tune your hearts and minds to the cadence of optimism, for in the days ahead, a wondrous opportunity awaits.

Life is a journey, and often, it presents us with crossroads where choices define our destiny. The path that unfolds before you is not just a walkway; it's a tapestry of chances, challenges, and triumphs. It's a canvas where your actions paint the portrait of your future. The days ahead hold a promise – a promise of growth, of learning, and of a wondrous opportunity that could transform your aspirations into achievements.

As you stand on the precipice of the unknown, remember this: preparation is the key that unlocks the door to success. Be prepared, not just with tools and skills, but with a mindset forged in resilience and a heart fueled by passion. Opportunities are elusive, often disguised as challenges or wrapped in the cloak of hard work. Embrace the hurdles, for behind each one lies a stepping stone toward greatness.

In the vast landscape of the digital age, where every click and keystroke shapes our online existence, search engine optimization (SEO) is the compass that guides us through the virtual wilderness. Imagine your dreams as a website waiting to be discovered by the world. Now, more than ever, it is crucial to optimize your path to success, ensuring that your journey is not just seen but celebrated.

So, when I say, "Be prepared to accept a wondrous opportunity in the days ahead," I'm urging you to fine-tune your digital presence, to make your mark on the global stage. The internet is the gateway to the future, and with strategic SEO, you can amplify your voice, your vision, and your impact.

But, let's not forget the human element – the connections we forge, the relationships we nurture. In the days ahead, remember that success is not a solitary journey. It's a collaborative dance where every partner adds their unique flair. Network, communicate, and support one another. Together, we can create a symphony of success that resonates far beyond the confines of individual achievement.

In conclusion, my friends, as you prepare to embark on the journey ahead, let the phrase "Be prepared to accept a wondrous opportunity in the days ahead" echo in your thoughts. The days ahead are not just a passage of time; they are a treasure trove of chances waiting to be uncovered. Be bold, be prepared, and be ready to embrace the wondrous opportunity that awaits you.

Thank you, and may your days ahead be filled with triumphs, growth, and the sweet symphony of success.

WONDROUS OPPORTUNITY

LEARN CHINESE - Today
今(jīn)天(tiān)
Lucky Numbers 45, 37, 51, 15, 14, 47

37

The dice

> If you are afraid to shake the dice, you will never throw a six.

Fortune Cookie Fam, gather 'round! Today's message is a challenge wrapped in a sweet treat: **"If you are afraid to shake the dice, you will never throw a six."** Now, this isn't about gambling or luck; it's about **taking a chance on yourself**. It's a call to action that echoes within the pages of Fortune Cookie Coaching.

Let's face it, we all get scared. Maybe you're yearning to launch that business idea but fear of failure holds you back. Perhaps that dream promotion seems just out of reach, leaving you hesitant to even apply.

But here's the thing: **great things rarely happen in our comfort zones.** Fortune Cookie Coaching reminds us that **growth requires action**. When you shy away from taking a chance, you guarantee one outcome – stagnation.

Shaking the dice represents taking that leap of faith. It's about embracing the unknown, putting yourself out there, and actively chasing your goals. Here's why it's worth it:

- **Even small steps lead to progress:** Every action, however seemingly insignificant, moves you closer to your dreams.
- **Failure is a stepping stone:** Setbacks are inevitable, but they are also opportunities to learn and adapt.
- **The only true failure is inaction:** When you don't try, you guarantee you won't succeed.

But Fortune Cookie Coaching doesn't just tell you to jump – it equips you to **land safely**. This book provides the tools to:

- **Develop a risk-assessment framework:** Analyze potential challenges, create contingency plans, and manage your fear.
- **Build a support system:** Surround yourself with people who believe in you and can offer guidance.
- **Celebrate small wins:** Acknowledge your progress, no matter how small, to keep yourself motivated.

Remember, Fortune Cookie Fam, every success story began with a leap of faith. **Shaking the dice** doesn't guarantee a "six," but it makes it a possibility. And even if you don't roll the highest number this time, you'll gain valuable experience, move closer to your goals, and discover a strength you never knew you had.

So, Fortune Cookie Fam, what are you waiting for? Stop clinging to the sidelines! **Embrace the uncertainty, shake the dice, and roll the bones on your dreams!** Fortune Cookie Coaching is your guide on this journey of self-discovery and audacious action. Go forth, be bold, and **create a life filled with possibility!**

4 20 27 29 36 40

Lucky numbers

38

Tomorrow

Tomorrow you will find the item you have been searching for.

Esteemed readers of "Fortune Cookie Coaching,"

As we gather here, our hearts open like pages of possibility. Today, I present to you a phrase—a whisper from the universe: **"Tomorrow you will find the item you have been searching for."**

Let us unwrap this cosmic gift together:

1. **The Quest of the Heart**: Imagine life as a grand scavenger hunt. We seek treasures—some tangible, others ethereal. Perhaps you've been searching for love, purpose, or a missing puzzle piece. Tomorrow, the universe conspires: "Your quest nears its end."
2. **The Lost and Found**: We've all misplaced something—a key, a memory, a dream. But what if life's cosmic custodian holds our lost items? Tomorrow, check the lost-and-found bin of destiny. You might find not just keys, but answers.
3. **The Map of Synchronicity**: Tomorrow isn't random; it's a coordinate

on your soul's map. The item you seek—its longitude and latitude—are etched in stardust. Pay attention to signs—the stranger's smile, the song on the radio. They're breadcrumbs leading home.

4. **The Invisible Threads**: Sometimes, we search for tangible things—a book, a necklace. But often, we seek intangibles—peace, belonging, forgiveness. These are the cosmic items—the ones that rearrange constellations within us.
5. **The Whispering Wind**: Tomorrow, listen. The wind carries secrets—the location of buried treasures. It rustles leaves, nudging you toward the item you've yearned for. Trust its whispers; they're coded messages.
6. **The Serendipity Café**: Imagine a café where serendipity serves coffee. Tomorrow, visit. Sit by the window, sip warmth, and watch. The person at the next table—the one reading your favorite book—might hold your item. Strike up a conversation; the universe loves dialogue.
7. **The Quantum Leap**: Tomorrow, leap. Not physically, but mentally. Shift your frequency. Believe that the item exists—whether it's a lost love, a career breakthrough, or a forgotten melody. Quantum physics says: Your belief collapses the wave function into reality.
8. **The Cosmic Auction**: Picture a celestial auction house. Tomorrow, attend. The auctioneer raises the gavel—the item you seek is up for bidding. What's your currency? Hope? Persistence? Bid generously; the universe rewards earnest seekers.
9. **The Keymaster**: Tomorrow, meet the Keymaster. They guard doors—the ones that lead to your item. They're disguised as strangers, mentors, or unexpected opportunities. When they offer a key, accept. It fits a hidden lock.
10. **The Final Revelation**: As we conclude, remember: Tomorrow isn't just a day; it's a treasure chest. Open it with reverence. Seek not just with eyes, but with wonder. The item you find might not be what you expected—it might be better.

"Tomorrow you will find the item you have been searching for." – Unknown

TOMORROW

May your quest be fruitful, your heart open, and your steps guided toward cosmic reunions. ✨

LEARN CHINESE - Beverage; drink
饮(yǐn)料(liào)

Lucky Numbers 5, 33, 2, 18, 9, 15

39

Un sourire

 Un sourire fait disparaître
tous les soucis.
1 13 21 39 40 48

Mesdames et Messieurs, chers amis, bonjour!
Aujourd'hui, je suis ravi de vous adresser la parole sur un sujet qui transcende les frontières de la motivation personnelle : le pouvoir incommensurable d'un sourire. Comme le dit si justement l'adage, "Un sourire fait disparaître tous les soucis". C'est bien plus qu'une simple expression ; c'est une vérité universelle qui résonne au plus profond de nous.

Imaginez un monde où chaque visage rayonne de positivité, où chaque regard est empreint de bienveillance. Un monde où les défis et les soucis, aussi imposants soient-ils, s'effacent devant la lumière éclatante d'un simple sourire. C'est un monde que nous pouvons créer, un monde où l'optimisme est la force motrice qui guide nos actions.

Chaque jour, nous faisons face à des obstacles, des défis et des moments difficiles. Mais souvenons-nous que notre attitude envers ces défis peut faire toute la différence. Un sourire, c'est comme une clé secrète qui ouvre les portes de la résilience et de la persévérance. C'est un geste simple, mais d'une puissance extraordinaire.

En tant que professionnels, entrepreneurs, étudiants, ou tout simplement en tant qu'êtres humains, cultivons l'habitude de sourire face à l'adversité. Non seulement cela transformera notre propre perspective, mais cela influencera positivement ceux qui nous entourent. Le sourire est contagieux, et il crée un environnement propice à la croissance personnelle et collective.

Dans le domaine professionnel, le pouvoir du sourire ne doit pas être sous-estimé. Il crée des liens, renforce les équipes et favorise une atmosphère de travail positive. De plus, dans le contexte numérique d'aujourd'hui, où la visibilité en ligne est cruciale, n'oublions pas que même à travers nos écrans, un sourire sincère peut transcender les barrières virtuelles et créer une connexion authentique.

Alors, engageons-nous à faire de chaque jour une occasion de répandre la joie et l'optimisme. Partageons des sourires, élevons-nous mutuellement et construisons un avenir où les défis ne sont que des opportunités déguisées. Rappelez-vous toujours : "Un sourire fait disparaître tous les soucis". C'est une philosophie de vie qui peut transformer notre monde, un sourire à la fois.

Je vous encourage tous à adopter cette vision positive, à être les architectes d'un changement qui commence par un geste aussi simple qu'un sourire. Ensemble, cultivons un monde où la lumière de l'optimisme chasse les ténèbres des soucis. Merci.

8 11 22 30 31 48

Lucky Numbers

40

Dark room

> *Following other's path is like entering a dark room without light.*

L adies and gentlemen, esteemed readers of "Fortune Cookie Coaching," welcome.

Today, I want to share a simple yet profound truth that has the power to ignite the flames of inspiration within each of us: "Following other's path is like entering a dark room without light." These words encapsulate the essence of individuality, the magic of carving your own journey, and the limitless potential that lies within your unique footsteps.

Imagine, for a moment, entering a room enveloped in darkness, devoid of any guiding light. That room represents the path chosen by others — a path that might not align with your passions, dreams, and aspirations. It's a path that, in the absence of your authentic light, leaves you stumbling in the shadows of someone else's vision.

Each one of us is a unique spark in the grand tapestry of existence. We are not meant to blend into the darkness by treading the same worn-out trails.

Instead, we are destined to be beacons of light, casting our brilliance onto unexplored paths and creating a legacy uniquely our own.

In the era of social media, it's easy to be captivated by the seemingly glamorous lives and successes of others. But remember, those stories are the highlights, not the whole journey. What makes your journey extraordinary is not found in mimicking someone else's script but in the authentic narrative you write for yourself.

Embracing your individuality is not only liberating for you but also inspirational for others. It's a testament to the courage it takes to venture into the unknown, to dance to the beat of your own drum, and to shine your light even in the darkest corners. Your uniqueness is a gift to the world, a contribution to the symphony of diverse voices that collectively create a masterpiece.

Think of the great innovators, the visionaries, the game-changers throughout history. They didn't find their way by following the paths of others; they forged new trails, explored uncharted territories, and embraced the uncertainty of the journey. The darkness they faced became the canvas upon which they painted their brightest ideas and most profound successes.

So, my friends, let the phrase "Following other's path is like entering a dark room without light" be your guiding star. It is a call to authenticity, a reminder that your light, your passion, your dreams are the beacons that will illuminate your path and inspire others to embark on their own extraordinary journeys.

In the grand tapestry of life, your unique thread weaves a story that has never been told before. Cherish it, embrace it, and let it guide you towards the extraordinary. Today, as you stand on the precipice of your own greatness, remember: Your light is not only for you but for the world that awaits the brilliance only you can bring.

Thank you for being the unique, extraordinary individuals you are. May your journey be as bright as the light you carry within.

Go forth and shine.

Thank you.

FORTUNE COOKIE COACHING

LEARN CHINESE - To taste
尝(cháng)一(yī)尝(cháng)
Lucky Numbers 25, 36, 8, 47, 15, 46

41

New possibilities

Investigate new possibilities with friends. Now is the time!

L adies and gentlemen, esteemed readers of "Fortune Cookie Coaching," welcome.
    Today, I stand before you not just as an individual, but as a collective force bound together by the ties of friendship and a shared commitment to personal growth. In the tapestry of life, we often find ourselves at crossroads, presented with the opportunity to shape our destinies and explore uncharted territories. Today, I bring to you a simple yet profound message: "Investigate new possibilities with friends. Now is the time!"

Life is an intricate dance, a series of moments woven together by the choices we make. Each decision opens up a new path, and often, the most enriching journeys are those taken in the company of friends. It is said that the quality of our lives is determined by the quality of our relationships, and what better way to enhance our lives than by embarking on new adventures with those we hold dear?

The world is a vast canvas of opportunities, waiting to be explored and experienced. But the true magic happens when we decide to venture into the unknown with the companionship of friends. Together, we become a formidable force, capable of conquering challenges and savoring the sweet taste of success. The bonds we share with our friends are like bridges that connect us to new horizons, and it is on these bridges that we discover the strength of unity and the joy of shared accomplishments.

Now is the time to cast away the shackles of hesitation and embrace the spirit of exploration. Our friends are not just companions on this journey; they are the pillars of support, the confidants who inspire us to reach for the stars. Together, we can turn dreams into reality and transform aspirations into achievements.

Investigating new possibilities is not merely a call to action; it is an invitation to growth, resilience, and the fulfillment of our potential. When we stand side by side with our friends, the challenges that once seemed insurmountable become stepping stones to greatness. The shared laughter, the shared struggles, and the shared victories forge bonds that withstand the tests of time.

So, my friends, let us pledge to investigate new possibilities together. Let us dare to dream big and aspire to achieve even bigger. In the tapestry of our lives, let each thread represent a shared adventure, a collective triumph, and a memory that binds us forever. Now is the time to turn the page, to embrace the unknown with open hearts and willing spirits.

As we embark on this journey together, let the spirit of camaraderie guide us, and let the echoes of our shared laughter resonate through the corridors of time. Invest in the power of friendship, explore the vast landscapes of possibility, and seize the opportunities that await. Now is the time, my friends—our time to shine, to grow, and to create a tapestry of memories that will forever define the beauty of our shared existence.

Thank you, and let the adventure begin!

NEW POSSIBILITIES

2 9 31 38 44 47

Lucky Numbers

42

Darkness

> *Darkness cannot drive out darkness; only light can do that.*

Ladies and gentlemen, esteemed readers of "Fortune Cookie Coaching," welcome.

Today, we gather here not just as individuals, but as a collective force, united by a common purpose - the pursuit of light in the face of darkness. As we stand on the threshold of our dreams, let us be reminded of the profound truth encapsulated in the words of the great Martin Luther King Jr.: "Darkness cannot drive out darkness; only light can do that."

In a world often shrouded in challenges, uncertainties, and adversity, it is easy to succumb to the shadows that threaten to engulf our spirits. But, my friends, it is precisely in these moments of darkness that the power of light becomes most potent. Think about it: a single flame can pierce through the thickest veil of night, illuminating the path ahead. So too can the light within each and every one of us dispel the gloom that may surround us.

Each of you carries a unique brilliance, a radiant light that has the potential to transform not only your own life but also the lives of those around you. It's a light fueled by passion, purpose, and the unwavering belief that, despite the challenges we face, there is always hope. It's a light that, when shared, can create a beacon of inspiration for others, guiding them through their own moments of darkness.

In the journey towards our goals and aspirations, let us not be daunted by the shadows of doubt or the storms of adversity. Instead, let us be beacons of positivity, beacons of resilience, beacons of light. For it is through our collective radiance that we can create a tapestry of hope and inspiration that transcends individual triumphs and resonates throughout our communities, our nations, and the world.

Remember, it is not enough to simply bemoan the darkness; we must actively choose to bring forth the light. In every action, every decision, and every interaction, let the brilliance within you shine. Embrace the challenges as opportunities for growth, and let the flames of your determination burn even brighter in the face of adversity.

As we embark on this journey together, let us be guided by the understanding that our collective light has the power to drive out the darkness that seeks to envelop us. Let us stand united, a force of positivity and change, and let our actions be a testament to the enduring truth: darkness cannot drive out darkness; only light can do that.

So, my friends, let your light shine, bright and unwavering. Illuminate the world with your passion, kindness, and resilience. Together, we can overcome any darkness that may come our way and forge a path towards a brighter, more hopeful future.

Thank you, and may your light inspire greatness in all that you do.

您將得到一個意外的驚喜。

43

Superior person

> The superior person is modest in his speech but exceeds in action.

Esteemed readers of "Fortune Cookie Coaching,"

Today, I stand before you as a guide—a lantern bearer on your path toward well-being. Our lives are woven with threads of choices, and today, we unravel the wisdom behind the phrase: **"The superior person is modest in his speech but exceeds in action."**

1. **The Power of Humble Words**: Imagine words as seeds—tiny, unassuming. When planted with care, they grow into mighty oaks. The superior person knows this. They speak with humility, avoiding grandiose claims or empty boasts. Their words are like gentle rain, nurturing the soil for deeds to flourish.
2. **The Symphony of Silence**: Modesty in speech isn't silence; it's a symphony. The superior person listens more than they speak. They absorb others' melodies—their hopes, fears, dreams. And when they

do speak, it's purposeful. Like a maestro, they conduct conversations with grace.

3. **The Art of Understatement**: Have you noticed how the moon whispers its presence? It doesn't shout, yet its glow moves oceans. Similarly, the superior person understates. They don't need applause; their actions resonate louder. They say, "I'll try" instead of "I can." And then they exceed.
4. **The Canvas of Actions**: Imagine speech as a canvas. Words paint strokes, but actions create masterpieces. The superior person wields both brush and chisel. They promise less and deliver more. When they say, "I'll be there," they arrive early. When they say, "I care," they prove it through kindness.
5. **The Dance of Integrity**: Modesty isn't weakness; it's integrity. The superior person aligns words with deeds. They don't promise what they can't fulfill. Their commitments are solid, like oak beams supporting bridges. When they say, "I'll help," they roll up their sleeves.
6. **The Ripple Effect**: Imagine a pebble dropped in a pond. Ripples spread, touching distant shores. The superior person's actions are those ripples. They volunteer quietly, mentor generously, uplift silently. Their impact isn't measured in decibels; it's felt in hearts.
7. **The Legacy of Service**: The superior person doesn't seek applause; they seek impact. They know that deeds outlive speeches. When they see a need, they act. When they encounter suffering, they alleviate it. Their legacy isn't etched in marble; it's woven into lives touched.
8. **The Compass of Purpose**: Modesty isn't about playing small; it's about aiming high. The superior person knows their purpose—the North Star guiding their actions. They climb mountains, not to shout from the peak, but to breathe rarefied air and bring back wisdom.
9. **The Invitation to Others**: The superior person inspires without fanfare. Their actions beckon others to greatness. When they build bridges, they invite others to cross. When they plant trees, they invite others to rest in their shade. Their humility is magnetic.
10. **The Oath of Excellence**: Imagine a silent oath taken by the superior

person: "I'll be better today than yesterday." They don't shout it; they live it. Their actions—small and consistent—accumulate into excellence. They exceed not for applause, but because it's who they are.

"The superior person is modest in his speech but exceeds in action." – Confucius

May your words be gentle, your deeds mighty, and your legacy profound. As you step into the world, remember: The banquet of life awaits, and your actions are the feast. ☆🎴

5 18 28 29 40 49

Lucky numbers

44

Taxes and fines

> A fine is a tax for doing wrong. A tax is a fine for doing well.

Esteemed readers of "Fortune Cookie Coaching,"

Today, I stand before you as a guide—a lantern bearer on your path toward well-being. Our lives are woven with threads of choices, and today, we unravel the wisdom behind the phrase: **"A fine is a tax for doing wrong. A tax is a fine for doing well."**

1. **The Paradox of Justice**: Imagine life as a courtroom. In one corner stands Justice, blindfolded, weighing deeds on her scales. In the other corner, we—the players in this cosmic drama. The phrase reminds us that life's ledger balances both virtue and transgression. When we err, we pay a fine—a reckoning for our missteps. But when we excel, we pay a tax—a tribute to our competence, our diligence, our very excellence.
2. **The Fine Print**: Let's dissect this paradox. A fine—often punitive—penalizes deviation from norms. It's the parking ticket, the late fee, the consequence for crossing boundaries. But what about the tax? Ah,

the tax—it's the silent applause for doing well. It's the nod from the universe, acknowledging our efforts. When we excel, we're taxed—not with burden, but with recognition.

3. **The Currency of Effort**: Imagine effort as currency. Every endeavor—whether small or grand—adds to our account. When we falter, we withdraw from this balance. The fine reminds us: "You've overdrawn." But when we thrive, the tax replenishes our coffers. It's the interest earned on our hard work.

4. **The Art of Doing Well**: What does it mean to "do well"? It's not just financial success; it's mastery. It's the pianist's nimble fingers, the gardener's blooming roses, the parent's bedtime story. Doing well is craftsmanship—the alchemy of turning sweat into gold. And for this, we're taxed—not with gold coins, but with fulfillment.

5. **The Fine Line**: The phrase dances on a tightrope—a fine line between right and wrong, success and failure. It whispers: "Balance is key." When we stumble, we learn. When we soar, we share. The fine and the tax—they coexist, like yin and yang. Embrace both.

6. **The Tax Collector**: Who collects our taxes? Not the IRS, but life itself. It tallies our deeds—the whispered kindness, the midnight oil burned, the courage to leap. And when we've done well, life stamps our passport with approval. We cross borders—from mediocrity to excellence.

7. **The Fine Forgiveness**: Sometimes, fines are forgiven. We learn, we grow, and the slate is wiped clean. But taxes? They accumulate. The more we do well, the richer we become—not in material wealth, but in character.

8. **The Legacy of Excellence**: Imagine a lineage of excellence—a tapestry woven by generations. Our ancestors paid taxes—through sweat, sacrifice, and resilience. They built bridges, composed symphonies, healed wounds. Their legacy whispers: "Do well, for you inherit our treasury."

9. **The Invitation**: Today, I invite you to embrace both fine and tax. When you stumble, learn. When you excel, celebrate. Pay your dues—humbly, gratefully. And remember: The banquet of life awaits. Savor each course.

10. **The Final Transaction**: As we conclude, let's settle accounts. The fine? It's forgiven. The tax? It's yours to claim. Go forth, dear readers, and do well. The universe awaits your tax return.

"A fine is a tax for doing wrong. A tax is a fine for doing well." – Unknown
May your balance sheet be rich, your heart full, and your legacy golden.
🌟💰

您將避過一件嚴重的麻煩事。

45

Friendship

Seek friendship and you will find someone special this month.

Esteemed readers of "Fortune Cookie Coaching,"

As we gather here, our hearts open like fortune cookies, ready to reveal the wisdom hidden within. Today, I present to you a phrase that dances between hope and serendipity: **"Seek friendship and you will find someone special this month."**

1. **The Quest for Connection**: Imagine life as a grand treasure hunt. We seek gold, but what if the real treasure lies in human hearts? Friendship—the golden thread that binds us across time and space. This month, let's embark on a quest: to seek, to connect, and to discover someone special.
2. **The Art of Seeking**: Seeking isn't passive; it's an art. Like a compass, our hearts point toward kindred souls. We attend gatherings, join clubs, swipe through profiles. But true seeking isn't about quantity; it's about

quality. Seek with intention, not haste.

3. **The Magic of Intention**: Intention is our wand—the spell that summons connections. When we seek friendship, we cast a spell of openness. We say, "I see you." And in that recognition, we find magic—the spark that ignites special bonds.

4. **The Serendipity of Timing**: Fate whispers, "This is your moment." Perhaps it's a chance encounter at a coffee shop, a shared laugh in a crowded room, or a virtual hello across continents. Trust the timing; it's divine choreography.

5. **The Friendships We Deserve**: Seek not just anyone, but those who mirror your soul. Seek the listeners, the laugh-sharers, the midnight confidantes. Seek those who celebrate your quirks, who see your scars as constellations.

6. **The Dance of Vulnerability**: Seeking friendship requires vulnerability—the courage to say, "I'm here." It's the dance of revealing our stories—the messy chapters, the triumphant verses. Vulnerability is the bridge to special connections.

7. **The Language of Presence**: Seek not just with words, but with presence. Be fully there—eyes wide, heart open. Listen to their laughter, their fears, their dreams. In presence, we find the extraordinary in the ordinary.

8. **The Special Ones**: Who are the special ones? They're the ones who remember your favorite song, who send random texts just to say, "I'm thinking of you." They're the ones who hold your secrets like precious gems.

9. **The Ripple Effect**: Friendship isn't solitary; it's a ripple. When we find someone special, the ripples extend. They touch others—our families, our communities. Friendship is the butterfly flapping its wings, creating storms of love.

10. **The Invitation**: As this month unfolds, seek. Seek with curiosity, with wonder. Seek not just for yourself, but for the world. For when we find someone special, we become special too—a constellation in each other's skies.

"**Seek friendship and you will find someone special this month.**" – **Unknown**

May your seeking be fruitful, your connections magical, and your heart forever open. 🌟🌸

4 9 19 22 32 45

Lucky numbers

46

Real estate and stocks

You will do better in real estate than in stocks.

Fortune Cookie Fam, listen up! Today's message is a doozy: **"You will do better in real estate than in stocks."** Now, this isn't a one-size-fits-all prophecy. But it is a nudge to consider a powerful path – real estate investing.

Before we dive in, let's acknowledge the wisdom of Fortune Cookie Coaching. This book isn't about stock-picking or fortune-telling. It's about **building a strong financial foundation**. And real estate can be a **powerful tool** in your arsenal.

Here's why "You will do better in real estate than in stocks" might hold weight for YOU:

- **Tangible Asset:** Unlike stocks, a property is something you can see, touch, and even live in (if you choose!).
- **Potential for Growth:** Real estate can appreciate in value over time, offering long-term gains.
- **Passive Income:** Renting out a property creates a steady stream of

income, potentially giving you more freedom.
- **Control & Leverage:** You can make improvements to your property, influencing its value directly. Leverage financing allows you to control a larger asset with less upfront capital.

However, remember, real estate isn't a magic bullet. It requires **research, effort, and smart decision-making**. But with the guidance from Fortune Cookie Coaching, you can approach real estate with confidence:

- **Educate Yourself:** Learn about different investment strategies, market trends, and local regulations.
- **Seek Guidance:** Consider working with a real estate agent or financial advisor.
- **Start Small:** Don't jump in headfirst. Consider smaller investment properties or partnering with others.
- **Do Your Numbers:** Carefully analyze costs, potential returns, and long-term commitment.

Now, here's the key takeaway: **this fortune cookie isn't telling you to ditch stocks altogether**. It's whispering the potential of adding real estate to your investment portfolio.

Remember, Fortune Cookie Coaching is your guide to building a **diversified financial future**. Explore all options, weigh the risks and rewards, and choose the path that aligns with your goals and risk tolerance.

So, Fortune Cookie Fam, is real estate your calling? Maybe, maybe not! But with the knowledge you gain from this book, you can make informed decisions about your financial future. Go forth, explore your options, and build a wealth-building strategy that empowers you! Remember, the key to success is **knowledge, action, and a healthy sprinkle of fortune cookie wisdom!**

Learn Chinese — bookstore
书店　　*shu dian*

47

Success

You will win success in whatever you attempt.

Ignite Your Soul, Seize the Day: YOU Will Win Success!
    Ladies and gentlemen, esteemed readers of "Fortune Cookie Coaching," welcome.

Friends, dreamers, doers! The air crackles with possibility today. Let it energize your very core, for within each of you lies a burning ember of brilliance waiting to ignite. You, yes YOU, are on the precipice of something magnificent. A canvas stretches before you, vast and white, primed for the masterpiece of your dreams.

But doubt may whisper, insidiously slithering into your ear, "What if I fail? What if it's too big, too bold, too audacious?"

Silence that voice! For it is a liar, a thief of potential. Instead, **listen to the thunderous roar of your own ambition.** Hear the symphony of your passion. Feel the ground tremble beneath your feet as you take that first, fearless step.

Forget the limitations others may try to impose. Their yardsticks are too short, their horizons too narrow. **YOU define your own measure of success.** It's not a gilded trophy on a shelf, but the fire in your belly, the joy in the journey, the impact you make on the world around you.

You are not alone in this arena of dreams. Look around you. See the spark in every eye, the tremor in every hand. We are a collective force, each with a unique flame to contribute to the blaze of progress. Let's ignite it together!

There will be stumbles, yes, moments of darkness and doubt. But remember, darkness is merely the absence of light. **Your resolve, your tenacity, your unyielding faith – these are the torches that will light your way.** Let setbacks be fuel, not extinguishers. Learn, adapt, rise stronger.

And never, ever forget this: YOu will win success in whatever you attempt. Not because of some preordained destiny, but because of the indomitable spirit that resides within you. It is the spirit that whispers, "I will try," the spirit that shouts, "I will overcome," the spirit that roars, "I will achieve!"

So, my friends, let this day be the day you unleash your fire! Let your ambitions soar like eagles, let your actions thunder like storms, let your heart beat with the rhythm of unyielding purpose.

This is your time, your stage, your masterpiece. Paint it with passion, sculpt it with perseverance, and illuminate it with the unwavering belief that **YOU will win success.**

Go forth, dreamers, doers, achievers! The world awaits your light!

10 21 22 25 40 48

Lucky Numbers

48

Passionate relationships

> *You form passionate relationships without compromising your independence.*

Embrace Connection: A Symphony of Self and Spirit

Ladies and gentlemen, esteemed readers of "Fortune Cookie Coaching," welcome.

Look around! Faces lit with the energy of a thousand stars, hearts pounding with the rhythm of ambition and hope. We stand here, not as a scattered chorus, but as a symphony – each instrument unique, yet harmonizing in the melody of life. Yet, sometimes, in this grand orchestra, we find ourselves playing a silent solo, yearning for connection while clinging to the comfort of solitude.

Friends, I say: break free from that solo act! This world craves the richness of your melody, the fire in your soul. You were not born to echo chambers, but to ignite dance floors, to inspire symphonies of your own. But remember, this liberation doesn't demand the surrender of your own tune. You, yes YOU, are a masterpiece in progress, an ever-evolving composition of dreams and desires. And in this symphony of self, independence is not a lonely exile, but the fertile ground from which passionate relationships bloom.

Imagine it: forming bonds that crackle with shared passions, where laughter rings like cymbals and whispered secrets dance like wind chimes. Imagine collaborating with kindred spirits, your unique melodies intertwining to create a symphony grander than any heard before. This, my friends, is the magic of genuine connection, nurtured by the strength of your own rhythm.

But be warned, this harmony demands courage. It demands vulnerability, the willingness to share your melody, knowing it might clash, might falter. Yet, in that risk lies the reward. For when two independent souls find their rhythm together, the music soars. It builds you up, amplifies your dreams, and reminds you that you are never truly alone.

So, step out of the shadows, let your inner maestro loose! Dance with strangers, harmonize with friends, and above all, never compromise the melody that makes you YOU. In this symphony of life, your independence is not an obstacle to connection, but its very foundation. For it is from the strength of your solo that the most powerful duets are born.

Go forth, ignite your soul, embrace connection! Let your independence be the bridge, not the barrier, and together, let's compose a symphony that echoes through the ages!

LEARN CHINESE - Taste

口 (kǒu) 味 (wèi)

Lucky Numbers 54, 12, 43, 30, 17, 16

49

Right doors

Don't wait for others to open the right doors for you.

Open Your Own Doors: A Motivational Speech to Forge Your Path

Ladies and gentlemen, esteemed readers of "Fortune Cookie Coaching," welcome.

Friends, gather close! Let's cast aside the cobwebs of doubt and ignite the fire of possibility within! For too long, we've been lulled into a passive stance, waiting for someone, anyone, to crack open the door to our dreams. But what if I told you that **the key has been in your pocket all along?**

Don't wait for others to open the right doors for you.

Instead, **become the architect of your own destiny!** Bust down the flimsy facades of expectation and **build a fortress of your own making, brick by brick, dream by dream.**

This isn't a call to recklessness, but a clarion cry for conscious creation.

We are not marionettes, dancing to the whims of fate. We are the sculptors, the painters, the **artists of our own lives!**

Think of the greatest minds in history. Did they wait for permission to paint the Sistine Chapel, write the Declaration of Independence, or launch a rocket into the cosmos? No! They **carved their own paths,** leaving behind a legacy of audacious action.

We are all capable of such audacity. We have the power to **ignite the spark of passion within,** to **fan the flames of curiosity,** and to **chase the whispers of our wildest dreams.**

But the journey begins with a single step. A step outside our comfort zones. A step towards the unknown. A step fueled by the unwavering belief that **we are the authors of our own stories.**

So, let's rewrite the narrative! Let's trade in the passive voice for the active. Let's **shatter the glass ceilings of expectation and soar on the wings of our own potential!**

Here's your manifesto:

- **Embrace the power of "I can."** Replace doubt with determination, fear with fire.
- **Turn your setbacks into stepping stones.** Learn from every stumble, rise from every fall.
- **Don't be afraid to color outside the lines.** The most vibrant masterpieces often defy convention.
- **Surround yourself with dreamers, not doubters.** Seek inspiration, not stagnation.
- **Celebrate the small victories.** Each step forward is a testament to your strength.

Remember, the world is your canvas, and your dreams are the brushstrokes. Don't wait for someone to hand you the paintbrush. **Pick it up yourself!**

Go forth, friends, and paint your masterpiece! Open the doors that beckon you, build the bridges that connect you to your goals, and **let your light shine so bright that it illuminates the path for others to follow.**

The world awaits your unique brilliance. Don't make it wait any longer. Now, step outside and open the first door!

Remember, the greatest journey begins with a single step. Take yours today!

5 10 16 19 20 38

Lucky Numbers

50

Simplify your life

You simplify your life in many ways and find great rewards.

Simplify to Soar: Unclutter Your Life, Embrace the Extraordinary

Ladies and gentlemen, esteemed readers of "Fortune Cookie Coaching," welcome.

Friends, imagine a life. Not one weighed down by the clutter of "shoulds" and "maybes," but one sculpted by clarity and purpose. A life where the noise fades, and your own inner compass hums its true north. This, my friends, is the magic of *simplification*.

We live in a world that thrives on complexity. Schedules cram our days, notifications buzz in our pockets, and choices flood our every path. It's easy to feel like cogs in a machine, churning through the motions yet never quite finding traction. But within this whirlwind lies a profound truth: **in the act of simplifying, we reclaim our power.**

You simplify your life in many ways. It might be decluttering your physical space, letting go of possessions that no longer serve you. Or perhaps it's pruning your calendar, freeing time for passions long neglected. Maybe it's setting boundaries, protecting your energy from draining relationships and commitments.

Every step, however small, whispers a promise: **there's more to life than this.** And as you shed the unnecessary, the extraordinary emerges.

The rewards of simplification are vast, friends. You discover a newfound lightness, a mental and emotional space where creativity blossoms and dreams take root. You find yourself drawn to deeper connections, genuine conversations that nourish your soul. You wake up with purpose, your days no longer a blur of obligations, but a canvas for meaningful pursuits.

This isn't about deprivation, it's about liberation. It's about recognizing that true wealth lies not in what you own, but in what you experience. It's about prioritizing the moments that fill your heart, the connections that spark your soul, the pursuits that sing your unique song.

So, today, I challenge you to embrace the power of simplicity. Take a deep breath, look around, and ask yourself: "What can I let go of? What can I reclaim?" It might be a cluttered inbox, a toxic relationship, an endless to-do list. Whatever it is, release it. Make space for the extraordinary.

Remember, friends, **our lives are not meant to be deciphered, they're meant to be lived.** So simplify, savor, and soar. Let the world know the light that shines within you, unburdened and free. This is your time, your journey, your story. **Write it boldly, beautifully, and with the liberating power of a life made simple.**

Go forth, simplify, and find your extraordinary!

有知識就是好，無知識就是不好。

51

Take chances

> *If you are never scared, embarassed or hurt, it means you never take chances.*

Embrace the Tremble: A Speech on Daring to Dream and Building a Remarkable Life

L adies and gentlemen, esteemed readers of "Fortune Cookie Coaching," welcome.
 Friends, dreamers, risk-takers! We stand here today at a crossroads – not of physical roads, but of possibilities. Before each of us stretches a vast landscape of potential, shimmering with unlived moments and untangled triumphs. It's a breathtaking vista, isn't it? But as we gaze upon it, a curious truth emerges: **the path toward those glorious possibilities is rarely paved with comfort.**

Oh, how easy it would be to stay on the familiar track, where shadows of doubt don't linger and the sting of failure is a forgotten friend. Yet, in that safe haven, our dreams would remain mere figments, whispers in the wind instead of roaring symphonies in our souls.

Why? Because, my friends, **if you are never scared, embarrassed, or hurt, it means you never take chances.** It means you never step outside your comfort zone, never dance on the edge of the unknown, never truly **live.**

Fear may whisper in your ear, painting vivid pictures of missteps and stumbles. But remember, fear is merely a guard dog, barking warnings before venturing into the uncharted. Instead of cowering behind the fence, let's train that dog to walk beside us, a vigilant companion urging us to be cautious, not craven.

Embarrassment may sting like a summer sunburn, but just like that sunburn, it fades eventually. And let's be honest, haven't we all had enough embarrassing moments to fill a comic book anthology? They become badges of courage, proof that we dared to stand out, to put ourselves out there, to **dream bigger than our comfort zones.**

Hurt may leave scars, yes, but those scars become maps, etched with the lessons learned and the battles fought. They remind us of our resilience, our capacity to weather storms and emerge stronger, **wiser versions of ourselves.**

So, let's not shrink back from the trembles in our knees, the blushes on our cheeks, or the tears that well up. Let's see them as invitations to the grandest adventure, the one where we **embrace the uncertainty, forge our own path, and build a life truly remarkable.**

Remember, the world needs your daring, your audacity, your heart on fire with possibilities. Step into the light, embrace the tremble, and let your dreams become the soundtrack of your remarkable journey. **Go forth, risk-takers, and change the world!**

Share your dreams, encourage others to take risks, and celebrate the journey together!

TAKE CHANCES

9 16 17 30 37 42

Lucky Numbers

52

The rainbow and the rain

> **If you want the rainbow, you have to tolerate the rain.**

Embrace the Downpour: Unlocking the Rainbows Within

Ladies and gentlemen, esteemed readers of "Fortune Cookie Coaching," welcome.

Friends, gather close! Today, we stand not beneath a clear sky, but under a veil of rain. And yes, it might be tempting to hunker down, to wait for the clouds to part and reveal a sun-kissed rainbow. But what if I told you the rainbow you seek thrives not just after the rain, but *within* it?

"If you want the rainbow," a wise soul once said, "you have to tolerate the rain." This isn't about passively enduring hardship. It's about dancing in the downpour, learning to see the beauty woven into its very drops. It's recognizing that the rain nourishes the ground, quenches the thirsty earth, and washes away the dust, preparing the canvas for the vibrant hues to come.

Imagine the gardener who yearns for blooming roses. Does she curse the storm that whips the delicate buds? No, she understands its role in coaxing out the fragrance, in strengthening the stems. She trusts the process, knowing the sun will return, painting the world anew.

So, too, must we face our own storms. The entrepreneur facing setbacks, the artist battling self-doubt, the student drowning in doubts – all stand under the same downpour. Yet, it's within these very struggles that resilience is forged, creativity sparks, and character shines.

Think of the sculptor chipping away at the stone, not to escape the rough form, but to reveal the masterpiece hidden within. Each stroke, each tear of raindrop on his brow, brings him closer to the breathtaking beauty waiting to be unearthed.

Remember, friends, the rainbow doesn't magically appear after the rain is gone. It's born from the very interaction of sunlight and raindrops, a vibrant tapestry woven from both light and shadow. So, don't shy away from the downpour. Let it wash away your fears, quench your doubts, and nourish your spirit.

Embrace the challenges, the setbacks, the tears. For within them lies the potential for breathtaking triumphs, dazzling displays of your own inner rainbow. So, step out, arms outstretched, and welcome the rain. Let it dance on your skin, whisper its secrets in your ear, and know this: **the most magnificent rainbows only emerge after the storm.**

This, my friends, is not just a speech, it's a battle cry. Let it echo in your hearts, a reminder that you are the sculptor, the gardener, the artist of your own life. The rainbow awaits, painted not just on the canvas of the sky, but in the very depths of your being. Go forth, embrace the rain, and **unleash the rainbow within!**

LEARN CHINESE - Beer

啤(pí)酒(jiŭ)

Lucky Numbers 43, 22, 36, 18, 54, 38

53

Bounded by the Sky

☺ You are only bounded by the sky.
24 29 3 35 36 6

Beyond the Horizon: A Speech to Ignite Your Limitless Potential

Ladies and gentlemen, esteemed readers of "Fortune Cookie Coaching," welcome.

Friends, dreamers, doers! Look around you. We stand here, not on solid ground, but on the precipice of infinite possibility. Yes, there are walls, challenges, and whispers of doubt. But I say to you, with eyes open to the vast expanse above, **you are only bounded by the sky!**

Imagine it: a canvas of cerulean blue, boundless and free. That, my friends, is the canvas of your potential. No paintbrush is too bold, no dream too daring. Let the doubters clutch their fear like worn blankets, but you, you shed them like chrysalis wings and **soar on the thermals of ambition!**

Remember, the Wright brothers didn't build a cage, they built wings. Their vision wasn't limited by gravity, but by the horizon. And what did they find?

Not just flight, but a new dawn for humanity. **So, what is your horizon?** Is it a promotion, a masterpiece, a revolution in your field? Whatever it is, let it **ignite a fire in your soul** that no headwind can extinguish.

The path won't be easy. There will be storms, turbulence, and moments when the ground calls, tempting you to retreat. But listen, heroes are not forged in comfort. They are tempered by trials, shaped by resilience, and defined by the **unyielding pursuit of their dreams.**

You are capable of more than you know. You have within you the power to defy the odds, to rewrite the narrative. Don't let fear be your pilot. Grab the controls, chart your course, and **dance with the unknown!** Embrace the stumbles, learn from the falls, and rise, again and again, with the wings of determination spread wide.

Remember, **the sky is not the limit, it's the starting line.** Go beyond. Push past the comfort zone. Dare to paint your own masterpiece on the canvas of possibility. Leave your mark on the world, not with doubt and timidity, but with the vibrant strokes of passion, courage, and **audacious dreams!**

And when you reach your summit, don't be tempted to stay. Remember, the greatest view is not from the peak, but from the next climb. So, keep climbing, keep dreaming, keep **reaching for the sky!**

Let this be the day you break free from your self-imposed shackles. Let this be the day you declare, with unwavering conviction: "I am limitless, and my potential knows no bounds!"

Go forth, and paint your own sky!

☺ You are only bounded by the sky.
24 29 3 35 36 6

Lucky Numbers

54

Successful in Business

☺ **You will be unusually successful in business.**☺

Dear readers of "Fortune Cookie Coaching",

Today, I want to share with you a phrase that I recently found in a fortune cookie: "**You will be unusually successful in business**". This phrase is not just a prediction, but a powerful affirmation that can inspire and motivate you to reach new heights in your professional life.

Success in business is not just about making profits or expanding market share. It's about creating value, making a difference, and leaving a lasting impact. It's about innovation, leadership, and resilience. It's about learning from failures, embracing change, and pursuing your passion.

When we say, "You will be unusually successful in business", we are talking about a success that goes beyond the ordinary. We are talking about a success that sets you apart, that makes you unique. We are talking about a success that is not just about what you achieve, but how you achieve it.

This kind of success requires an unusual approach. It requires you to think differently, to challenge the status quo, to take risks. It requires you to be bold, to be creative, to be persistent. It requires you to have a vision, to set goals, and to work tirelessly towards them.

But remember, this journey to success is not a solo endeavor. It's about building relationships, fostering teamwork, and creating a culture of excellence. It's about inspiring others, empowering them, and helping them grow.

So, as you navigate your way in the world of business, keep this fortune cookie phrase in mind. Let it be your guiding light, your source of inspiration. Let it remind you that you are capable of achieving unusual success, that you have the potential to make a difference, that you have the power to create a legacy.

Believe in yourself, believe in your dreams, believe in your ability to succeed. And remember, success is not just about reaching your destination, it's about enjoying the journey.

With warm regards, Your Personal Coach

您心胸开阔，社交活跃。

55

Investment opportunity

AN INVESTMENT OPPORTUNITY WILL BE PROFITABLE FOR YOU.

Dear readers of "Fortune Cookie Coaching,"

Today, I want to share with you a message of abundance, prosperity, and boundless potential—a message that holds the promise of financial success and freedom: "All investment opportunity will be profitable for you."

What a powerful affirmation! What an exciting reminder that the universe is conspiring in your favor, aligning the stars and paving the way for success and abundance in your financial endeavors. In a world that often presents us with challenges and uncertainties, there is something truly empowering about the prospect of every investment opportunity leading to profitability and prosperity.

But here's the thing about investment opportunities—they're not just about financial gain. They're also about investing in yourself, in your dreams, and in your vision for the future. Whether it's investing in your education, your skills, or your passions, every investment you make has the potential to yield dividends far beyond the realm of money.

So why is it important to embrace the promise of profitable investment opportunities? Because when you do, you step into a mindset of abundance, possibility, and limitless potential. You no longer see obstacles as barriers, but rather as opportunities for growth and expansion. You trust in your ability to make wise decisions, take calculated risks, and create the life of your dreams.

But profitable investment opportunities aren't just about luck or chance—they're also about preparation, research, and taking strategic action. It's about doing your due diligence, seeking out opportunities that align with your values and goals, and being willing to step outside your comfort zone in pursuit of your dreams.

So as you continue your journey through the pages of "Fortune Cookie Coaching," I encourage you to hold onto this powerful affirmation: "All investment opportunity will be profitable for you." Let it be a reminder to trust in your intuition, to take bold action, and to seize every opportunity that comes your way with confidence and determination.

Thank you, dear reader, for your willingness to embrace the promise of profitable investment opportunities in your life. And may you continue to invest in yourself, in your dreams, and in your vision for the future with unwavering faith and determination.

Thank you, and may your journey be filled with abundance, prosperity, and endless opportunities for growth and success.

2 3 24 28 32 44

Lucky numbers

56

Love and happiness

You will always be surrounded with love and happiness.

Fortune Cookie Fam, gather 'round! Today's message isn't just a sweet treat, it's a beautiful promise: **"You will always be surrounded with love and happiness."** Now, Fortune Cookie Coaching knows life isn't all sunshine and rainbows, but here's the secret: happiness isn't a destination, it's a journey we cultivate.

This little message reminds you of the **unwavering love** that exists in your life, even when times get tough. It could be the love of your family, the unwavering support of friends, or the quiet comfort of a pet. Remember, Fortune Cookie Coaching emphasizes the importance of building strong relationships – these connections are a powerful source of love and happiness.

Here's how you can **cultivate more love and happiness** in your life:

- **Practice gratitude:** Take time each day to appreciate the good things in your life, big and small. Gratitude fosters a positive outlook and attracts more happiness.

- **Nurture your relationships:** Invest time and energy into the connections that matter most. Show your loved ones you care through acts of kindness and words of affirmation.
- **Spread the love:** Random acts of kindness, a helping hand to a neighbor, or a smile to a stranger create a ripple effect of positive energy. You can't control the world, but you can control the energy you bring to it.
- **Embrace the present moment:** Don't dwell on the past or worry about the future. Savor the present moment, find joy in everyday experiences, and appreciate the beauty around you.
- **Live a life of purpose:** When you're working towards something bigger than yourself, it creates a sense of meaning and fulfillment, contributing significantly to happiness.

Remember, Fortune Cookie Coaching is your guide to building a fulfilling life. This book equips you with tools to strengthen your relationships, cultivate gratitude, and find purpose.

Love and happiness are already within you, and they are all around you. Sometimes, all it takes is a gentle nudge to recognize them. So, Fortune Cookie Fam, go forth and **cultivate the love and happiness in your life!** Share it with others, and watch your world blossom in unexpected ways. Remember, you are worthy of love and happiness, and you have the power to create it, every single day!

您心胸開阔，社交活躍。

57

Beauty

Beauty is its various forms appeals to you.

Lucky # 19, 30, 59, 22, 21, 9
Learn Chinese: Son, Zi, 子

Beauty Beyond the Surface: A Call to Find Your Brilliance

L adies and gentlemen, esteemed readers of "Fortune Cookie Coaching," welcome.
Friends, dreamers, seekers of wonder!
Gather close, for I bring a message not of polished perfection, but of the dazzling kaleidoscope of beauty that lives in every one of us. Forget the narrow lens of conventional standards, the airbrushed ideals that flicker on screens. **Today, we celebrate the raw, unfiltered magnificence of being uniquely alive!**

Yes, **"beauty in its various forms appeals to you,"** and that includes you, yes you, standing right there! Look around – in the fiery spark of a child's curiosity, in the weathered hands that tell stories of toil and triumph, in the symphony of languages that paint our world with vibrant voices. Beauty hides in the unexpected, in the quirk of your smile, the glint of passion in your eyes, the way your mind dances with ideas.

Don't let anyone tell you your light is too dim, your melody too off-key. The world craves the authenticity you bring, the tapestry woven from your experiences, your dreams, your scars.

Live your own life, friends! Optimize your spirit for joy, for kindness, for the relentless pursuit of what ignites your soul. Let compassion be your keyword, let courage be your meta description. Rise above the algorithms of comparison, the search queries of self-doubt. You are not a trend, a hashtag, a fleeting click. You are an original masterpiece, waiting to be unveiled.

So, go forth, unapologetically you! Paint your canvas with vibrant hues of laughter, vulnerability, and resilience. Let your imperfections become brushstrokes of character, your struggles the fertile ground where strength blossoms. Embrace the cracks, the crevices, the unexpected twists that make you who you are.

Remember, the world needs your unique light, your untamed symphony. Don't dim your brilliance to fit someone else's search criteria. **Be loud, be bold, be the impossible algorithm that breaks the mold!** Show the world the beauty that truly matters, the beauty that lies within, waiting to be unleashed.

Go forth, and shine!

Beauty is its various forms appeals to you.

Lucky # 19, 30, 59, 22, 21, 9
Learn Chinese: Son, Zi, 子

58

Equals

> *Force equals too much; effort equals too little; being equals enough.*

Friends, dreamers, doers!

Ladies and gentlemen, esteemed readers of "Fortune Cookie Coaching," welcome.

Do you ever feel like the world asks you to be a **bulldozer**? Charging through life, shoulders back, muscles tight, pushing, shoving, aiming for that ever-distant finish line? We're told to hustle, to grind, to **force** our way to success. But friends, I'm here to tell you: **Force equals too much.**

It burns us out, leaves us frayed and hollow. It turns our dreams into deadlines, our passions into pressure. We end up pushing boulders uphill, forgetting to **enjoy the climb.**

Then there's the other side of the coin: the path of **least resistance.** We **effortlessly** drift through life, letting the current carry us, content with mediocrity. We convince ourselves that ambition is exhausting, that striving is foolish. But friends, **effort equals too little.**

It leaves us unfulfilled, yearning for something more. It makes us strangers to our own potential, content with echoes instead of symphonies. We end up floating downstream, never feeling the thrill of navigating rapids or exploring hidden tributaries.

So, where do we find the sweet spot? Where does ambition meet joy, and perseverance dance with ease? The answer, my friends, is in **being**. In showing up, fully present, with hearts open and minds curious.

"**Being equals enough**" isn't about complacency; it's about **alignment.** It's about aligning your actions with your values, your desires with your dreams. It's about **stepping into the present moment** and letting your authentic self shine through.

Being means showing up for that early morning run with a smile, not a grimace. It means giving your all to your work, not just for the paycheck, but for the joy of creation. It means embracing challenges with open arms, knowing that growth lies beyond comfort.

Being means letting go of the need to control and trusting the flow of life. It means celebrating small victories and learning from big stumbles. It means accepting yourself, flaws and all, and knowing that you are **enough, just as you are.**

So, my friends, ditch the bulldozer and the inflatable pool float. Step onto the solid ground of your own being. Embrace the dance of ambition and ease, of effort and grace. Remember, **force equals too much; effort equals too little; being equals enough.** And when you do, you'll find that the greatest victories come not from pushing or drifting, but from simply **being present, authentic, and true to yourself.**

Now go forth, and be enough! Be extraordinary! Be **you.** The world needs your unique light, not your tired muscles or passive drift. And remember, we're all in this together, on this beautiful, messy, magnificent journey called life.

Let's be enough, together.

您將得到一個意外的驚喜。

59

Trust others

Trust others, but still keep your eyes open.

Esteemed readers of "Fortune Cookie Coaching,"

Today, I invite you to explore a delicate balance—a dance between trust and discernment. Our lives are woven with relationships, opportunities, and encounters. And within this intricate tapestry, the phrase **"Trust others, but still keep your eyes open"** emerges as a guiding star.

Let us unravel its wisdom:

1. **The Art of Trust**: Trust is the currency of human connection. It's the bridge that spans hearts, the glue that binds teams, and the foundation of partnerships. When you trust, you extend an olive branch—a silent invitation for others to meet you halfway. Trust is the fertile soil where relationships bloom.
2. **The Vulnerability Paradox**: Trust requires vulnerability. It's like stepping onto a tightrope, knowing that the net might not catch you.

But therein lies the paradox: Vulnerability isn't weakness; it's courage. When you trust, you risk disappointment, yet you also open the door to profound connections.

3. **Eyes Wide Open**: Trust doesn't mean blind acceptance. Keep your eyes open, not in suspicion, but in awareness. Observe actions, listen to words, and discern intentions. Trust isn't a free pass; it's an ongoing assessment. As Maya Angelou wisely said, "When someone shows you who they are, believe them the first time."

4. **The Compass of Intuition**: Your intuition is a compass—trust it. Sometimes, it whispers caution when all seems well. Pay attention. Trust isn't about ignoring warning signs; it's about honoring your inner knowing. Trust your gut; it's often wiser than your mind.

5. **Forgiveness and Boundaries**: Trust doesn't mean overlooking betrayal. When trust is broken, forgiveness becomes the path to healing. But forgiveness doesn't negate boundaries. Set healthy limits. Trust doesn't mean handing over your heart without discernment.

6. **The Ripple Effect**: Trust isn't solitary; it ripples outward. When you trust, you inspire trust in return. Your openness encourages others to reveal their authentic selves. Trust becomes a chain reaction—a force that transforms communities, workplaces, and families.

7. **Trust in Leadership**: As leaders, trust is our currency. Trust your team; empower them. Trust isn't micromanagement; it's delegation with confidence. When you trust, you create an environment where innovation thrives, and loyalty blossoms.

8. **The Gift of Second Chances**: Trust allows for redemption. People stumble; they falter. But sometimes, they rise stronger. Give second chances—not blindly, but with discernment. Remember, even the moon wanes before it waxes.

9. **The Dance of Authenticity**: Trust flourishes in authenticity. Be genuine; show your imperfections. Authenticity invites trust because it says, "I'm real, flaws and all." When you're authentic, you invite others to be the same.

10. **The Legacy of Trust**: Trust isn't fleeting; it's a legacy. When you trust,

you leave footprints in hearts. Your impact extends beyond your lifetime. Trust becomes a gift you bestow upon the world.

In closing, dear readers, may you trust with eyes wide open—like a sailor navigating uncharted waters. May your heart remain open, yet discerning. For in this delicate balance lies the art of living fully.

"Trust others, but still keep your eyes open." – Unknown

May your journey be rich with trust, wisdom, and the courage to see both light and shadows. ⭐👀

Lucky Numbers 34, 35, 31, 53, 21, 25

60

Error and truth

From error to error, one discovers the entire truth.

Embrace the Error, Unveil the Truth:

Ladies and gentlemen, esteemed readers of "Fortune Cookie Coaching," welcome.

Today we celebrate the dance of discovery, the exhilarating stumble through shadows towards illumination. Today, we raise a toast to the unsung hero of progress: the glorious, messy, oh-so-human **error**.

Yes, you heard me right. Error, that crimson splash on the pristine canvas of perfection, that unexpected turn on the well-trodden path. Error, the whispered "oh no" that precedes the triumphant "aha!" Error, the fertile ground where failure blossoms into wisdom.

For too long, we've worshipped at the altar of infallibility, chasing unattainable ideals that leave us bruised and breathless. But what if the true path, the one painted in sun-dappled gold, lies not in a straight line, but in a glorious zig-zag of mistakes?

Imagine a scientist, pipette poised, hands trembling. One misplaced drop, a bubbling concoction unlike anything expected. Yet, within that unexpected brew, nestled the very answer they sought.

Imagine an artist, brush swirling, frustration mounting. A stroke too bold, a color clash so vibrant it makes your eyes sting. But in that dissonance, that break from the predictable, blooms a masterpiece never before conceived.

Imagine a climber, fingers digging into rock, doubt gnawing at their core. A misstep, a jolt, a heart hammering against ribs. But with each precarious slip, with each scraped knee and bitten lip, they forge a path no map could ever reveal.

Friends, the truth is not a singular beacon in the distance. It's a kaleidoscope of fragments, each unearthed through the stumbles and scrambles of our journey. From error to error, we inch closer, piecing together the grand mosaic of understanding.

So let us shed the shackles of perfectionism! Let us celebrate the glorious messiness of being human! Let our "mistakes" become brushstrokes in the masterpiece of our lives.

Embrace the detours, the stumbles, the unexpected turns. For in the labyrinth of error, in the dance of trial and correction, lies the key to unlocking a truth far richer, far more dazzling than any we could ever imagine from a standing start.

Go forth, dear friends, and stumble with purpose. Fall with grace, for in the rising, you will find not just your footing, but a truth so vast, so vibrant, it will set your very soul ablaze. Remember, from error to error, we discover the entire truth, and in that truth, we discover ourselves.

Now, let the errors commence! Let the failures become fertilizer! Let the journey begin!

5 18 28 29 40 49

Lucky Numbers

61

Cooperative people

> People in your surroundings will be more cooperative than usual.

Unlocking Unprecedented Cooperation

Ladies and gentlemen, esteemed readers of "Fortune Cookie Coaching," welcome.

Can you feel that hum in the air? It's a current of anticipation, a whisper of opportunity that crackles around us like lightning just begging to strike. Today, the stars align not just for personal triumphs, but for something grander, something collective. Today, we stand on the precipice of **unprecedented cooperation**!

Think about it! The universe, in its infinite wisdom, has seen fit to **clear the path for collaboration**. People in your surroundings, your colleagues, your neighbors, even your rivals, will find themselves surprisingly open to your ideas, receptive to your hand outstretched in partnership. This, my friends, is not merely chance; it's a cosmic nudge, a cosmic "Go big!" scrawled across the sky.

But cooperation, like a fire, needs a spark. And that spark, that catalyst, must come from you. From your unwavering belief in the impossible, from your infectious enthusiasm, from your audacious vision that refuses to be dimmed. Look within, find that spark, and fan it into a roaring inferno. Let it illuminate the path not just for yourself, but for those around you.

Now is the time to **step outside your comfort zones**, to reach across divides, to build bridges where walls once stood. Let go of preconceived notions, of skepticism, of the limiting voices that whisper "It can't be done." Instead, embrace the open minds, the willing hands, the unexpected alliances that this unique moment offers. Together, we can achieve what seemed unimaginable, paint a future brighter than any solo brushstroke could ever envision.

Remember, collaboration isn't about sacrificing your individuality; it's about amplifying it. It's about weaving your dreams into a tapestry so rich, so vibrant, that it inspires the whole world to pick up a thread and join the creation.

So, go forth, my friends, with your spark ablaze. Speak your truth, share your vision, and invite others to co-create the masterpiece that is waiting to be born. Remember, **people are waiting to cooperate**. This is your moment, your symphony, your masterpiece. Conduct it with courage, with passion, and with the unshakeable belief that together, we can rewrite the stars themselves!

Let the fire of cooperation burn bright, and let its light guide us to a future of shared triumph, a future where collaboration reigns supreme! Thank you, and let's go make the impossible inevitable!

FORTUNE COOKIE COACHING

LEARN CHINESE - Beverage; drink
饮(yǐn)料(liào)
Lucky Numbers 5, 33, 2, 18, 9, 15

62

Original ideas

Your original ideas find a place in your work and play.

Ladies and gentlemen, esteemed readers of "Fortune Cookie Coaching," welcome.

Let's ignite a fire under our creativity today. Let's cast aside the mundane and embrace the power within a single, electrifying phrase: **"Your original ideas find a place in your work and play."**

Think about it. Within each of us lies a wellspring of unique thoughts, perspectives, and solutions. They simmer just beneath the surface, waiting to be tapped. But often, fear, self-doubt, or the humdrum of routine muffle our spark. We settle for the expected, the safe, the "been done before."

But what if we dared to unleash our originality? What if we believed, truly believed, that our ideas belonged, not just in the quiet corners of our minds, but woven into the very fabric of our lives?

Imagine your workday transformed. No more autopilot tasks, no more cookie-cutter solutions. Instead, you approach each challenge with a fresh lens, proposing innovative ideas that invigorate yourself and your colleagues. Your passion becomes palpable, drawing others into your contagious enthusiasm.

Now, step outside the office. Hobbies become vibrant playgrounds for experimentation. Whether it's reimagining your garden, composing a quirky song, or crafting a unique recipe, your unique touch elevates the ordinary into the extraordinary. You leave your mark on the world, however small, and in doing so, enrich your own experience.

Remember, originality isn't about grand inventions or earth-shattering discoveries. It's about bringing your authentic self to everything you do. It's about infusing your world with the vibrant colors of your imagination.

So, silence the inner critic, banish the fear of failure. Embrace the messy, imperfect process of creation. Start small. Experiment. Play! Remember, even the most dazzling masterpieces began with a single, hesitant brushstroke.

Here's the secret: The world craves your originality. It needs your perspective, your unique solutions, your spark of joy. Don't wait for permission. Don't let fear hold you back. Start today, right now, to infuse your work and play with the magic of your own ideas. Remember, **your original ideas have a place, and the world is waiting to be surprised.** Go forth, create, and shine!

10 19 26 27 37 42

Lucky Numbers

63

The effect you have

You are often unaware of the effect you have on others.

Esteemed readers of "Fortune Cookie Coaching,"

Today, I invite you to embark on a journey—a journey of self-awareness and impact. For within you lies a force, subtle yet profound, that shapes lives, kindles hope, and leaves indelible marks on the hearts of others. The phrase before us is a mirror—a reflection of your hidden power:

"You are unaware of the effect you have in others."

Let us unravel its layers, like petals unfurling in the morning sun:

1. **The Ripple Effect**: Imagine a pebble dropped into a still pond. Ripples radiate outward, touching distant shores. Your actions, too, create ripples—their impact extending far beyond your awareness. A smile shared with a stranger, a word of encouragement, a small act of kindness—they resonate, echoing through time.
2. **The Unseen Threads**: You move through life, weaving threads of

connection. Your laughter, your empathy, your presence—they bind souls. But often, you remain unaware—the quiet architect of bonds that strengthen families, heal wounds, and bridge divides.

3. **The Butterfly Wings**: Chaos theory speaks of the butterfly effect—a butterfly flapping its wings in Brazil causing a tornado in Texas. Similarly, your smallest gestures—listening attentively, offering solace—set off ripples of change. You are the butterfly, and your wings matter.
4. **The Echoes of Words**: Words—those delicate vessels—carry weight. When you speak, you release echoes into the universe. A compliment, a thank-you, a heartfelt apology—they linger, shaping destinies. You may forget, but others carry your words within them.
5. **The Silent Legacy**: Your legacy isn't etched in stone; it's whispered in memories. Think of mentors, teachers, friends who altered your course. You, too, leave footprints—the teacher who ignited curiosity, the friend who held your hand during storms. Your legacy blooms silently.
6. **The Power of Authenticity**: Authenticity is your superpower. When you show up as your true self—flaws and all—you grant permission to others. They, too, shed masks, revealing vulnerabilities. Your authenticity becomes a beacon, guiding lost ships to safe harbors.
7. **The Unseen Acts**: Not all heroes wear capes; some wear everyday clothes. You—unaware—perform heroic acts. A timely phone call, a handwritten note, a shared meal—they rescue sinking hearts. You are the unsung hero—the quiet lifeguard on life's shores.
8. **The Mirror of Empathy**: Empathy—the ability to step into another's shoes—is your magic mirror. When you listen without judgment, when you validate feelings, you gift empathy. It's a mirror that reflects back healing, compassion, and shared humanity.
9. **The Dance of Influence**: Influence isn't about grand speeches or titles; it's about presence. Your mere existence influences. Your resilience whispers, "You can overcome." Your kindness murmurs, "The world can be better." You are a living sermon.
10. **The Invitation**: As you turn these pages, remember: You are the ripple, the butterfly, the echo. Your effect is woven into the fabric of existence.

Seek not fame, but impact. Be aware, dear reader, for your smallest acts create galaxies.

"You are unaware of the effect you have in others."

May your awareness deepen, your heart expand, and your legacy be a symphony of kindness. ✨🌿

LEARN CHINESE - Strawberry
草(cǎo)莓(méi)
Lucky Numbers 20, 50, 38, 32, 52, 51

64

Your goals

Nothing can keep you from reaching your goals. Do it!

F ortune Cookie Fam, assemble! Today's message is a battle cry disguised in a sweet treat: **"Nothing can keep you from reaching your goals!"** Now, this isn't some mystical guarantee. Life throws curveballs, doubters appear, and challenges will arise. But this fortune cookie isn't about sunshine and rainbows – it's about **unleashing the power within you**.

Think about it. Goals aren't fleeting desires; they're **burning ambitions** that propel you forward. They give your life purpose, direction, and a sense of accomplishment. And while obstacles may appear, remember this: **you have the strength and resilience to overcome them.**

Here's the secret sauce: **belief**. When you truly believe in your ability to achieve your goals, mountains become molehills, and doubts become stepping stones. Fortune Cookie Coaching is your guide on this journey of self-belief. This book equips you with the tools to:

- **Craft clear and actionable goals:** Specificity is key! Define your goals, break them down into smaller steps, and set realistic timelines.
- **Develop unwavering determination:** Prepare for setbacks, anticipate challenges, and commit to pushing through even when things get tough.
- **Embrace a growth mindset:** Challenges are opportunities to learn and grow. Learn from mistakes, adapt your strategies, and keep moving forward.
- **Fuel your passion:** Passion is the fire that keeps you ignited. Stay connected to your "why" and let it be your driving force.

But remember, Fortune Cookie Fam, **you are not alone!** Surround yourself with supportive people who believe in you. Leverage the wisdom of Fortune Cookie Coaching, and use it to build a powerful support system – a team that celebrates your victories and lifts you up during setbacks.

This fortune cookie isn't a guarantee, it's a **declaration of empowerment**. It reminds you that **nothing can keep you from reaching your goals** except for one thing: yourself. So, silence the inner critic, unleash your potential, and grab those goals with unwavering determination! Remember, Fortune Cookie Fam, you are capable of achieving anything you set your mind to. Go forth, **be unstoppable, and make your dreams a reality!**

10 21 22 25 40 48

Lucky numbers

65

A banker

> *A banker is someone who lends you an umbrella when the sun is shining,*

Esteemed readers of "Fortune Cookie Coaching,"

Today, I stand before you as a guide—a lantern bearer on your path toward wisdom and insight. Our lives are woven with threads of metaphor, and today, we unravel the wisdom behind the phrase: **"A banker is someone who lends you an umbrella when the sun is shining."**

1. **The Paradox of Preparedness**: Imagine a sunny day—the sky a canvas of blue, the warmth embracing you. You step out, umbrella forgotten. But wait! Here comes the banker—an unexpected ally. They offer you an umbrella, not for rain, but for the unpredictable storms of life. The message? Be prepared, even when the sun smiles upon you.
2. **The Currency of Kindness**: The banker isn't just a financial guardian; they're a keeper of compassion. When they lend you that umbrella, they say, "I see you. I care." Their act transcends practicality—it's a gesture

of goodwill, a reminder that we're not alone in this vast universe.

3. **The Art of Anticipation**: Life mirrors seasons. Sunny days give way to thunderstorms. The banker knows this dance—the ebb and flow of fortune. They teach us to anticipate—not with fear, but with readiness. When the sun shines, gather your umbrellas—both literal and metaphorical.
4. **The Shelter of Friendship**: The umbrella isn't just a shield from rain; it's a symbol of protection. The banker's gift extends beyond weather—it's a promise: "I've got you covered." Likewise, seek friends who lend you emotional umbrellas—those who shield you from life's downpours.
5. **The Sunshine Within**: Sometimes, the sun hides behind clouds—the storms brewing within. The banker's umbrella isn't just for external weather; it's for the tempests of the heart. When you feel overwhelmed, reach out. Let others lend you their strength.
6. **The Generosity of Surplus**: The banker doesn't lend their only umbrella; they have extras. Likewise, generosity flows from abundance. When you share, it's not from scarcity, but from a wellspring of plenty. Be a banker—lend your umbrellas freely.
7. **The Unexpected Blessings**: Imagine the sun peeking through raindrops—the rainbow after the storm. The banker's umbrella isn't just practical; it's a harbinger of hope. When they lend it, they say, "This too shall pass." Embrace life's surprises—both sunny and rainy.
8. **The Invitation to Reciprocate**: The banker's act isn't a one-way street. Someday, you'll lend an umbrella—a hand, a smile, a listening ear. Pay it forward. Be the banker who brightens someone's day.
9. **The Eternal Sunshine**: The sun rises each day, even when hidden by clouds. The banker's umbrella isn't just for today; it's a promise for all tomorrows. Carry it with gratitude, knowing that kindness endures.
10. **The Final Forecast**: As we conclude, remember: Life isn't just about weathering storms; it's about sharing umbrellas. Be the banker—the one who lends not just umbrellas but also hope, kindness, and love.

"A banker is someone who lends you an umbrella when the sun is shining."

– **Unknown**

May your days be sunny, your friendships sturdy, and your heart ever ready to lend an umbrella. ☀☂

LEARN CHINESE - To catch a cold
感(gǎn)冒(mào)
Lucky Numbers 51, 5, 20, 50, 15, 55

66

Marketable ideas

You have the exceptional ability to understand the fancies of marketable ideas.

Unleash Your Marketable Magic: You Are an Idea Whisperer!

L adies and gentlemen, esteemed readers of "Fortune Cookie Coaching," welcome.
Today we embark on a journey to unlock a hidden superpower within you. It's a power that shimmers beneath the surface, waiting to be awakened: **the exceptional ability to understand the fancies of marketable ideas.**

Think about it. You interact with countless products, services, and experiences every day. But have you ever stopped to wonder what makes some ideas take flight while others fizzle out? It's not just about functionality or aesthetics; it's about understanding the unspoken desires, the hidden yearnings, the **fancies** that fuel consumer decisions.

And here's the exciting part: **you have the innate ability to tap into those fancies.** You see beyond the surface, sensing the emotional resonance, the cultural touchstones, the trends that simmer just below the radar. You're an **idea whisperer**, deciphering the language of the market with an uncanny intuition.

Now, imagine wielding this power with intention. You become the architect of captivating concepts, the alchemist who transforms ordinary ideas into marketable gold. You breathe life into products that resonate deeply with consumers, creating experiences that leave a lasting impact.

But how do you unleash this hidden potential? Here's your roadmap:

- **Embrace your curiosity:** Ask questions, delve deeper, understand the "why" behind consumer choices. What are their pain points? What are their aspirations?
- **Become an observer of the world:** Immerse yourself in culture, trends, and conversations. What are people talking about? What are they sharing? What are their unspoken desires?
- **Develop empathy:** Put yourself in the shoes of your target audience. Feel their joys, understand their frustrations, anticipate their needs.
- **Experiment and iterate:** Don't be afraid to test, fail, and refine your ideas. The market is a living organism; listen to its feedback and adapt accordingly.

Remember, your ability to understand the fancies of marketable ideas is not just a skill; it's a gift. It's the power to create positive change, to bring joy and value to people's lives, and to leave your unique mark on the world.

So, step out of the shadows, idea whisperers! Hone your intuition, flex your empathy muscles, and start weaving your magic. The world needs your unique perspective, your ability to translate desires into marketable realities. Go forth, **unleash your marketable magic**, and leave your mark on the world!

MARKETABLE IDEAS

LEARN CHINESE - Strawberry
草(cǎo)莓(méi)

Lucky Numbers 20, 50, 38, 32, 52, 51

67

Education, knowledge and action

The great aim of education is not knowledge but action.

L adies and gentlemen, esteemed readers of "Fortune Cookie Coaching," welcome.

Today, we gather to reflect upon a profound idea: "The great aim of education is not knowledge but action." This statement, attributed to the renowned educator Herbert Spencer, encapsulates a truth that resonates deeply with our pursuit of personal and collective growth.

Think about it for a moment. We spend years in classrooms, absorbing facts, theories, and concepts. We engage in rigorous study, striving to expand our minds and deepen our understanding of the world around us. Yet, education extends far beyond the confines of textbooks and lectures. True education transcends the mere accumulation of knowledge; it compels us to act upon what we learn.

Knowledge, in its purest form, is a powerful catalyst for change. It ignites our imagination, fuels our curiosity, and empowers us to envision a better tomorrow. But knowledge alone is not enough. It is through action that we transform our dreams into reality, that we turn our aspirations into achievements.

Imagine if the great thinkers and innovators of history had remained content with mere knowledge. What if Isaac Newton had simply pondered the concept of gravity without ever conducting his groundbreaking experiments? What if Marie Curie had kept her discoveries confined to the pages of her notebooks, never sharing them with the world?

The truth is, our potential lies dormant until we take that crucial step from knowing to doing. It is in the arena of action that we truly demonstrate our understanding, our passion, and our commitment to making a difference. Whether it's solving complex problems, advocating for social justice, or pursuing our personal goals, education empowers us to be agents of change in our own lives and in the world at large.

So, my friends, I urge you to embrace this profound truth as you continue your educational journey. Seek not only to expand your minds but also to enrich your lives through meaningful action. Let your knowledge be the springboard from which you leap fearlessly into the realm of possibility. Let your actions speak volumes about your dedication, your integrity, and your unwavering belief in the power of education to shape a brighter future.

Remember, the great aim of education is not simply to know, but to do—to inspire, to innovate, and to leave an indelible mark on the world. So go forth with courage and conviction, and may your actions reflect the boundless potential that lies within each and every one of you. Thank you.

5 26 30 32 37 41

Lucky Numbers

68

Write a letter

It's time to write a letter or email to one who is distant.

Ladies and gentlemen, esteemed readers of "Fortune Cookie Coaching," welcome.

Today, we gather to explore the profound power of connection, of reaching out to those who may be distant from us, whether in miles or in the depths of our hearts. The simple act of writing a letter or an email to someone who is far away carries with it a world of significance—a bridge across the chasm of distance, a lifeline of love and understanding, a beacon of hope in the darkness of separation.

In a world that often feels increasingly disconnected, where screens mediate our interactions and time zones stretch our relationships thin, it's easy to lose sight of the importance of human connection. Yet, it is precisely in these moments of separation, these instances of longing, that the power of reaching out becomes most apparent.

Think about someone in your life who you've been meaning to reconnect with—a friend from childhood, a mentor who guided you through a difficult time, a family member who's drifted away in the currents of life's busyness. Now imagine the impact of receiving a heartfelt letter or email from them, words penned with love and sincerity, reaching across the expanse to touch your heart.

Writing to someone who is distant is an act of courage, of vulnerability, of reaching out across the vastness of space and time to say, "You matter. Your presence in my life is significant. And even though we may be separated by miles or circumstances, our connection remains unbroken."

So I urge you, my friends, to take a moment today to pick up a pen or open your laptop and write that letter, compose that email. Let your words flow from the depths of your soul, expressing gratitude, sharing memories, offering support, or simply saying, "I'm here, and I care."

In doing so, you not only honor the bonds that connect us all but also reaffirm your own capacity for empathy, compassion, and love. And who knows? Your letter or email may be the very lifeline someone else desperately needs in this moment.

Remember, it's never too late to reach out, to extend a hand across the distance and remind someone that they are seen, they are heard, and they are loved. So let's seize this opportunity to write a letter or email to one who is distant, and in doing so, let's bridge the gap and strengthen the ties that bind us together as one human family. Thank you.

WRITE A LETTER

LEARN CHINESE - Beer

啤(pí)酒(jiǔ)

Lucky Numbers 43, 22, 36, 18, 54, 38

69

Good spirits

May the good spirits be with you always.

L adies and gentlemen, esteemed readers of "Fortune Cookie Coaching," welcome. Today, I invite you to embark on a journey of self-discovery, empowerment, and transformation guided by the timeless wisdom encapsulated in the phrase: "May the good spirits be with you always."

In a world filled with challenges, uncertainties, and moments of doubt, it's easy to lose sight of the abundant blessings that surround us. Yet, within each and every one of us lies the power to summon the good spirits—the positive energy, the resilience, the inner strength—that will guide us through life's twists and turns.

The phrase "May the good spirits be with you always" is not merely a wish or a hope; it is a reminder of the profound truth that we are never alone on this journey. Whether you call it fate, destiny, or simply the universe conspiring in your favor, there is a force greater than ourselves that is constantly working to uplift, support, and inspire us.

But here's the thing: tapping into the power of the good spirits requires intention, mindfulness, and a willingness to embrace the possibilities that lie beyond our perceived limitations. It's about cultivating a mindset of gratitude, compassion, and positivity, even in the face of adversity. It's about recognizing that every setback is an opportunity for growth, every challenge a chance to demonstrate our resilience, and every moment of darkness a potential for light to shine through.

So how do we invite the good spirits into our lives? It starts with a shift in perspective—a conscious decision to focus on the blessings rather than the burdens, the solutions rather than the problems, the opportunities rather than the obstacles. It means surrounding ourselves with people who lift us up, who believe in our potential, and who remind us of the goodness that resides within us.

It also means taking care of ourselves—mind, body, and soul—nourishing our spirits with practices that bring us joy, peace, and fulfillment. Whether it's meditation, exercise, creative expression, or acts of kindness towards others, each of us has the power to cultivate a sense of inner harmony that attracts the good spirits like a magnet.

So my friends, as you delve into the pages of "Fortune Cookie Coaching," may you be inspired to embrace the wisdom of this simple yet profound phrase: "May the good spirits be with you always." And may you carry its message in your hearts as you navigate the twists and turns of your own unique journey, knowing that you are never alone, that you are infinitely capable, and that the best is yet to come.

Thank you, and may the good spirits be with you always.

1 4 9 12 14 47

Fortune Numbers

70

Award

You will soon be awarded a great honor.

Dear readers of "Fortune Cookie Coaching,"
I stand before you today with a message of anticipation, excitement, and possibility. Within the pages of this remarkable book, you have encountered a phrase that holds the promise of greatness, the assurance of recognition, and the affirmation of your worth: "You will soon be awarded a great honor."

What a profound declaration! What a powerful reminder of the limitless potential that resides within each and every one of you. For in these words lies the invitation to step into your greatness, to embrace your unique gifts and talents, and to envision a future filled with achievement, fulfillment, and success.

But let me be clear: the honor that awaits you is not merely a matter of chance or luck. It is a reflection of your dedication, your perseverance, and your unwavering commitment to excellence. It is the culmination of countless hours of hard work, sacrifice, and determination. It is the recognition of the incredible value that you bring to the world each and every day.

So what does it mean to be awarded a great honor? It means seizing opportunities with courage and conviction, even in the face of uncertainty. It means trusting in your abilities and believing in your potential, even when others doubt you. It means staying true to your values and following your passion, even when the path ahead seems daunting.

But above all, being awarded a great honor is about embracing the journey—the highs and the lows, the victories and the setbacks—as essential components of your growth and evolution. It's about recognizing that true success is not measured by accolades or achievements, but by the impact you make on the lives of others and the legacy you leave behind.

So as you continue to journey through the pages of "Fortune Cookie Coaching," I encourage you to hold onto this powerful affirmation: "You will soon be awarded a great honor." Let it inspire you, let it motivate you, and let it remind you of the incredible potential that lies within you, waiting to be unleashed upon the world.

And when that moment of recognition finally arrives—when you stand before the world, honored and celebrated for your contributions—may you embrace it with humility, gratitude, and a profound sense of purpose. For you are destined for greatness, dear reader, and the world awaits the incredible impact that only you can make.

Thank you, and may you soon be awarded the great honor that you so richly deserve.

Learn Chinese — Chinese
中国的/汉语   *zhong guo de/han yu*

71

New and different

Try something new and different. You will like the results.

Dear readers of "Fortune Cookie Coaching,"

Today, I invite you to embark on a journey of discovery, growth, and transformation—one guided by the simple yet profound wisdom encapsulated in the phrase: "Try something new and different. You will like the results."

Think about it for a moment. How often do we find ourselves stuck in the rut of routine, clinging to familiarity and comfort, afraid to step outside of our comfort zones? Yet, it is precisely when we dare to venture into the unknown, to embrace the unfamiliar, that we unlock our true potential and experience the magic of new beginnings.

The phrase "Try something new and different" is not just a suggestion; it's an invitation to expand your horizons, to push the boundaries of what you thought possible, and to embrace the richness and diversity that life has to offer. It's about stepping out of your comfort zone, challenging yourself to grow, and opening yourself up to a world of endless possibilities.

NEW AND DIFFERENT

And here's the best part: you will like the results. Yes, change can be scary. Yes, it can be uncomfortable. But it is also incredibly rewarding. Whether it's learning a new skill, exploring a new hobby, or embarking on a new adventure, every step you take outside of your comfort zone brings you one step closer to the person you were meant to be.

So why wait? Why settle for the status quo when there's a whole world out there waiting to be discovered? As you delve into the pages of "Fortune Cookie Coaching," I encourage you to embrace the spirit of adventure, to seize every opportunity to try something new and different, and to trust in the process of growth and transformation.

And remember, dear reader, the results may surprise you. You may uncover hidden talents you never knew you had. You may forge connections with people who inspire and uplift you. You may even discover a newfound sense of purpose and passion that ignites your soul and propels you toward your dreams.

So go ahead, take that leap of faith, and try something new and different. I promise you won't regret it. And who knows? You may just find that the best is yet to come.

Thank you, and may your journey of exploration and discovery be filled with joy, wonder, and endless possibilities.

6 10 18 20 34 48

72

Always on our minds

☺ Don't forget, you are always on our minds. ☺
16 24 34 40 43 44

Dear readers of "Fortune Cookie Coaching,"
Today, I come to you with a message of reassurance, support, and unwavering belief in your potential. Within the pages of this remarkable book, you have encountered a phrase that carries with it the profound truth of your worth and significance: "Don't forget you are always on our minds."

What a powerful affirmation! What a beautiful reminder of the impact you have on the lives of those around you, and the indelible mark you leave on the world. In a universe that sometimes feels vast and indifferent, it's easy to lose sight of the fact that you are never alone—that there are people who care deeply about you, who believe in you, and who hold you in their thoughts and hearts every single day.

So often, we underestimate the power of our presence, the influence of our actions, and the ripple effect of our words. Yet, each and every one of you has the ability to touch lives, to inspire change, and to make a difference in ways both big and small. Whether it's a smile, a kind word, or a simple act of kindness, you have the power to brighten someone's day, to lift their spirits, and to remind them that they are not alone.

But here's the thing: being always on our minds is not just about the impact you have on others—it's also about recognizing the incredible value that you bring to the world simply by being yourself. It's about embracing your uniqueness, celebrating your strengths, and owning your worth with confidence and pride. It's about knowing that you are enough, exactly as you are, and that your presence in this world matters more than you could ever imagine.

So as you continue your journey through the pages of "Fortune Cookie Coaching," I encourage you to hold onto this powerful affirmation: "Don't forget you are always on our minds." Let it remind you of the love and support that surrounds you, even in the darkest of times. Let it inspire you to embrace your truest self and to live each day with purpose, passion, and authenticity.

And remember, dear reader, you are never alone. You are cherished, you are valued, and you are always on our minds.

Thank you, and may you continue to shine your light bright for all the world to see.

73

Plans

Be prepared to modify your plans.

Dear readers of "Fortune Cookie Coaching,"
 I stand before you today with a message of resilience, adaptability, and the power of embracing change. Within the pages of this insightful book, you've encountered a phrase that holds the key to navigating life's twists and turns with grace and determination: "Be prepared to modify your plans."

 Life, as we know, is unpredictable. It has a way of throwing unexpected challenges, detours, and curveballs our way, often when we least expect it. And in those moments, it's easy to feel overwhelmed, discouraged, or even defeated. But here's the truth: the ability to modify your plans—to adapt, to pivot, to embrace change—is not a sign of weakness, but rather a testament to your strength, resilience, and courage.

 Think about it. Some of the greatest achievements in history were born out of the willingness to modify plans in the face of adversity. Whether it's a last-minute change in strategy, a shift in perspective, or a complete overhaul of your original vision, every setback is an opportunity to reassess, to innovate, and to emerge stronger than ever before.

But modifying your plans is about more than just navigating obstacles; it's about embracing the beauty of the unknown, the excitement of new possibilities, and the freedom to chart your own course. It's about recognizing that sometimes the best-laid plans are meant to be revised, reimagined, and refined in order to align with your truest desires and aspirations.

So how do you prepare yourself to modify your plans? It starts with cultivating a mindset of flexibility, adaptability, and openness to change. It means letting go of rigid expectations and embracing the journey, with all its twists and turns, as an opportunity for growth and evolution.

It also means being proactive, staying nimble, and trusting in your ability to navigate whatever comes your way with courage and resilience. And most importantly, it means believing in yourself, in your capacity to overcome obstacles, and in the inherent wisdom of the universe to guide you towards your highest good.

So as you continue your journey through the pages of "Fortune Cookie Coaching," I encourage you to hold onto this powerful affirmation: "Be prepared to modify your plans." Let it serve as a reminder that no matter what challenges may arise, you have the strength, the resilience, and the determination to adapt and thrive.

Thank you, dear reader, for your courage, your tenacity, and your unwavering commitment to living a life of purpose and passion. And may you continue to embrace change with an open heart and a steadfast belief in the infinite possibilities that lie ahead.

Thank you, and may your journey be filled with endless opportunities for growth, fulfillment, and joy.

您心胸开阔，社交活跃。

74

Prosper

You could prosper in the field of entertainment.

Dear readers of "Fortune Cookie Coaching,"
Today, I come to you with a message of inspiration, possibility, and the boundless potential that resides within each and every one of you. Within the pages of this extraordinary book, you have encountered a phrase that carries with it the promise of greatness, the allure of creativity, and the excitement of pursuing your dreams: "You could prosper in the field of entertainment."

What a thrilling affirmation! What an invitation to explore your passions, unleash your talents, and step into the spotlight of your own unique brilliance. Whether you've always dreamed of gracing the silver screen, captivating audiences on stage, or expressing yourself through music, dance, or any other form of artistic expression, the field of entertainment beckons with endless opportunities for creativity, fulfillment, and success.

But here's the thing: thriving in the world of entertainment requires more than just talent—it requires dedication, perseverance, and an unwavering belief in yourself and your abilities. It's about honing your craft, pushing past your comfort zone, and embracing the challenges and triumphs that come with pursuing your passion.

So how do you prosper in the field of entertainment? It starts with a deep sense of self-awareness and a willingness to explore your unique gifts and talents. Take the time to discover what sets your soul on fire, what lights up your imagination, and what brings you the greatest joy and fulfillment. And once you've found your passion, don't be afraid to pursue it with everything you've got.

Next, surround yourself with mentors, coaches, and fellow artists who can support you, inspire you, and help you navigate the ins and outs of the entertainment industry. Learn from their experiences, seek their guidance, and never underestimate the power of community and collaboration in achieving your dreams.

And most importantly, never lose sight of your why—your reason for pursuing a career in entertainment. Whether it's to inspire others, evoke emotion, or simply to bring a little bit of joy and laughter into the world, let your passion be your guiding light as you navigate the highs and lows of this exhilarating journey.

So as you continue your exploration through the pages of "Fortune Cookie Coaching," I encourage you to hold onto this powerful affirmation: "You could prosper in the field of entertainment." Let it ignite your imagination, fuel your ambition, and embolden you to pursue your dreams with unwavering determination and unshakable faith.

Thank you, dear reader, for your courage, your creativity, and your commitment to bringing your unique gifts and talents to the world. And may you prosper abundantly in the field of entertainment, sharing your light and your love with audiences far and wide.

Thank you, and may your journey be filled with endless opportunities for growth, success, and fulfillment.

10 20 22 25 41 48

Lucky numbers

75

Respect for others

Your respect for others will be your ticket to success.

Dear readers of "Fortune Cookie Coaching,"
I stand before you today with a message of profound significance—a truth that has the power to shape not only your personal success but also your impact on the world around you. Within the pages of this remarkable book, you've encountered a phrase that holds the key to unlocking doors of opportunity, forging meaningful connections, and achieving your highest aspirations: "Your respect for others will be your ticket to success."

What a powerful affirmation! What a profound reminder of the importance of empathy, kindness, and integrity in our journey towards success. In a world that often values individual achievement above all else, it's easy to lose sight of the fact that true success is not measured solely by personal accolades or accomplishments, but by the relationships we build, the lives we touch, and the legacy we leave behind.

Respect for others is more than just a virtue; it's a guiding principle, a moral compass, and a foundation upon which we can build a life of meaning, purpose, and fulfillment. It's about recognizing the inherent dignity and worth of every individual, regardless of their background, beliefs, or circumstances. It's about treating others with kindness, empathy, and compassion, even when it's not easy or convenient to do so.

But here's the beauty of it: your respect for others isn't just a moral imperative—it's also your ticket to success. Whether you're pursuing your dreams in the boardroom, the classroom, or the world stage, the way you treat others speaks volumes about your character, your integrity, and your ability to lead with grace and humility.

Think about the most successful people you know—the ones who command respect, inspire loyalty, and leave a lasting impact wherever they go. Chances are, they're not just talented or ambitious; they're also deeply respectful of others, honoring their perspectives, valuing their contributions, and empowering them to reach their full potential.

So how do you cultivate respect for others as your ticket to success? It starts with a mindset shift—a conscious decision to approach every interaction, every relationship, with kindness, empathy, and an open heart. It means actively listening to others, seeking to understand their perspectives, and treating them with the same dignity and respect you would want for yourself.

It also means practicing humility, recognizing that true success is not a solo endeavor but a collaborative effort that requires the contributions and support of others. And most importantly, it means leading by example, embodying the values of respect, integrity, and kindness in everything you do, and inspiring others to do the same.

So as you continue your journey through the pages of "Fortune Cookie Coaching," I encourage you to hold onto this powerful affirmation: "Your respect for others will be your ticket to success." Let it guide your actions, shape your relationships, and pave the way for a future filled with abundance, fulfillment, and meaningful impact.

Thank you, dear reader, for your commitment to building a world where respect, kindness, and empathy are the currency of success. And may your journey be filled with endless opportunities to uplift, empower, and inspire

RESPECT FOR OTHERS

those around you.

Thank you, and may your respect for others lead you to the success you so richly deserve.

Learn Chinese — honey

蜂蜜 *feng mi*

76

Definition of life

Accept no other definition of your life, accept only your own.

Dear readers of "Fortune Cookie Coaching,"

Today, I come to you with a message of empowerment, self-discovery, and the incredible power that lies within each and every one of you. Within the pages of this transformative book, you have encountered a phrase that holds the key to unlocking your fullest potential and living a life of purpose, authenticity, and fulfillment: "Accept no other definition of your life, accept only your own."

What a profound affirmation! What a powerful reminder of the importance of owning your story, embracing your truth, and charting your own course in life. In a world that often seeks to define us by external standards, expectations, and opinions, it's easy to lose sight of the fact that the only definition of your life that truly matters is the one you create for yourself.

So often, we allow others to dictate the terms of our existence—to tell us who we should be, what we should do, and how we should live our lives. But here's the truth: you are the author of your own destiny, the architect of your own reality, and the master of your own fate. And the only limits that exist are the ones you place upon yourself.

Accepting no other definition of your life means honoring your dreams, your passions, and your deepest desires, even in the face of doubt, criticism, or adversity. It means trusting in your intuition, listening to the whispers of your heart, and following the path that lights you up from within.

But it also means embracing the journey—the ups and downs, the victories and setbacks—as essential components of your growth and evolution. It means recognizing that every experience, every challenge, is an opportunity for learning, for growth, and for becoming more fully aligned with your truest self.

So how do you accept only your own definition of your life? It starts with a commitment to authenticity—a willingness to show up as your most genuine, unapologetic self, even when it's not easy or comfortable to do so. It means embracing your strengths, your quirks, and your imperfections, and celebrating the unique gifts that only you can bring to the world.

It also means silencing the voices of doubt and negativity—whether they come from others or from within—and replacing them with a chorus of love, encouragement, and belief in your own worthiness. And most importantly, it means trusting in your own inner wisdom, your own intuition, and your own ability to create a life that is truly aligned with your highest vision of yourself.

So as you continue your journey through the pages of "Fortune Cookie Coaching," I encourage you to hold onto this powerful affirmation: "Accept no other definition of your life, accept only your own." Let it be your guiding light, your North Star, as you navigate the twists and turns of your unique path.

Thank you, dear reader, for your courage, your authenticity, and your unwavering commitment to living a life that is true to yourself. And may you continue to embrace your own definition of your life with courage, grace, and an unshakable belief in your own worthiness.

Thank you, and may your journey be filled with endless opportunities for growth, fulfillment, and joy.

FORTUNE COOKIE COACHING

Lucky Numbers 34, 56, 8, 17, 7, 1

77

Visit a park

Visit a park. Enjoy what nature has to offer.

Dear readers of "Fortune Cookie Coaching,"

Today, I stand before you with a gentle reminder—a call to reconnect with the beauty, the serenity, and the boundless wonder of the natural world that surrounds us. Within the pages of this transformative book, you've encountered a phrase that holds the promise of joy, renewal, and inspiration: "Visit a park. Enjoy what nature has to offer."

What a simple yet profound invitation! What a powerful reminder of the healing power, the rejuvenating energy, and the endless gifts that nature has to offer us. In a world filled with noise, distractions, and the constant hustle and bustle of modern life, it's easy to lose sight of the simple pleasures that await us in the great outdoors.

But here's the beauty of it: visiting a park isn't just about escaping the stresses of daily life—it's about reconnecting with ourselves, with each other, and with the natural world in a way that nourishes our souls and rejuvenates our spirits. It's about slowing down, breathing deeply, and immersing ourselves in the sights, sounds, and sensations of the natural world around us.

So why visit a park? Because in nature, we find solace. We find peace. We find a sense of belonging that reminds us of our place in the grand tapestry of life. Whether it's the gentle rustle of leaves in the breeze, the soothing babble of a babbling brook, or the vibrant colors of a sunset painting the sky, nature has a way of speaking to our hearts in a language that transcends words.

But visiting a park isn't just about enjoying the beauty of nature—it's also about reaping the countless benefits that come with spending time outdoors. Studies have shown that spending time in nature can lower stress levels, boost mood, and improve overall well-being. It can increase our creativity, our focus, and our ability to connect with others. And it can remind us of the importance of stewardship, of protecting and preserving the precious resources that sustain life on this planet.

So as you continue your journey through the pages of "Fortune Cookie Coaching," I encourage you to heed this simple yet powerful invitation: "Visit a park. Enjoy what nature has to offer." Let it be a reminder to prioritize self-care, to prioritize connection, and to prioritize the beauty and wonder that surround us each and every day.

Thank you, dear reader, for your willingness to embrace the healing power of nature and for your commitment to nurturing your mind, body, and spirit. And may your visits to the park be filled with moments of joy, wonder, and profound gratitude for the beauty of the natural world.

Thank you, and may your journey be filled with endless opportunities for growth, renewal, and connection.

Learn Chinese — Chinese
中国的/汉语　zhong guo de/han yu

78

Spirit of adventure

Let the spirit of adventure set the tone.

Dear readers of "Fortune Cookie Coaching,"

Today, I invite you to embark on a journey of self-discovery, growth, and boundless possibility—one guided by the exhilarating spirit of adventure. Within the pages of this transformative book, you've encountered a phrase that holds the power to ignite your imagination, awaken your curiosity, and propel you toward the extraordinary: "Let the spirit of adventure set the tone."

What an exhilarating invitation! What a powerful reminder of the magic, the excitement, and the endless opportunities that await us when we embrace the unknown with an open heart and a fearless spirit. In a world that often prizes routine, predictability, and comfort, it's easy to forget the thrill of stepping outside our comfort zones and embracing the exhilarating journey that lies beyond.

But here's the beauty of it: letting the spirit of adventure set the tone isn't just about seeking thrills or adrenaline rushes—it's about embracing life with a sense of wonder, curiosity, and openness to new experiences. It's about saying yes to the unknown, to the unexpected, and to the countless possibilities that lie on the horizon.

So why let the spirit of adventure set the tone? Because in adventure, we find growth. We find courage. We find a deeper understanding of ourselves and the world around us. Whether it's embarking on a solo backpacking trip through the mountains, trying a new cuisine, or learning a new skill, every adventure is an opportunity to expand our horizons, challenge our assumptions, and discover the depths of our own potential.

But letting the spirit of adventure set the tone isn't just about the big, bold moments—it's also about finding joy and excitement in the everyday. It's about approaching each day with a sense of curiosity and wonder, finding beauty in the small moments, and embracing the unexpected twists and turns of life with an open heart and a playful spirit.

So as you continue your journey through the pages of "Fortune Cookie Coaching," I encourage you to heed this powerful invitation: "Let the spirit of adventure set the tone." Let it be your guiding light, your North Star, as you navigate the ups and downs of life's incredible journey. Let it inspire you to embrace every opportunity, to seize every moment, and to live your life with passion, purpose, and an unwavering sense of adventure.

Thank you, dear reader, for your willingness to embrace the spirit of adventure and for your commitment to living a life filled with joy, excitement, and boundless possibility. And may your journey be filled with endless opportunities for growth, discovery, and unforgettable adventures.

Thank you, and may the spirit of adventure guide you toward the extraordinary life you were meant to live.

7 17 20 24 26 33

Lucky numbers

79

Purpose and direction

> *Efforts and courage are not enough without purpose and direction.*

Dear readers of "Fortune Cookie Coaching,"

I stand before you today with a message that cuts to the core of what it means to live a life of fulfillment, meaning, and impact. Within the pages of this transformative book, you've encountered a phrase that serves as a powerful reminder of the essential ingredients for success and fulfillment: "Efforts and courage are not enough without purpose and direction."

What a profound truth! What a powerful reminder of the importance of clarity, intention, and a sense of purpose in our journey towards achieving our dreams and creating a life that truly matters. In a world that often celebrates busyness, hustle, and achievement for achievement's sake, it's easy to lose sight of the deeper why—the driving force that gives meaning and direction to our efforts.

Efforts and courage are undoubtedly important—they are the fuel that propels us forward, the spark that ignites our passions, and the foundation upon which we build our dreams. But without purpose and direction, our efforts can become scattered, our courage can waver, and our dreams can lose their luster.

So why are purpose and direction so essential? Because they give meaning to our actions, clarity to our decisions, and a sense of fulfillment to our lives. They provide us with a roadmap—a guiding light that illuminates the path ahead and helps us navigate the inevitable challenges and setbacks we encounter along the way.

But finding purpose and direction isn't always easy—it requires introspection, self-awareness, and a willingness to dig deep and uncover what truly matters to us. It means asking ourselves the tough questions—What do I value most in life? What am I passionate about? What legacy do I want to leave behind?—and being willing to listen to the answers, even when they lead us down unexpected paths.

Once we've discovered our purpose, it's important to cultivate a sense of direction—a clear vision of where we want to go and how we plan to get there. This might involve setting goals, creating a plan of action, and surrounding ourselves with mentors, coaches, and supportive communities who can help us stay focused and accountable along the way.

So as you continue your journey through the pages of "Fortune Cookie Coaching," I encourage you to heed this powerful reminder: "Efforts and courage are not enough without purpose and direction." Let it inspire you to dig deep, to clarify your vision, and to take intentional action towards creating a life that aligns with your truest values and aspirations.

Thank you, dear reader, for your willingness to embark on this journey of self-discovery and growth. And may your efforts be guided by a clear sense of purpose and direction, leading you toward a future filled with meaning, fulfillment, and boundless possibility.

Thank you, and may you continue to courageously pursue your dreams with unwavering purpose and direction.

Learn Chinese — 18
十八　shi ba

80

Follow your heart

Follow your heart for success in the coming week.

Dear readers of "Fortune Cookie Coaching,"

As we embark upon a new week filled with endless possibilities and opportunities, I stand before you with a simple yet profound message—a guiding principle that has the power to transform your days, your weeks, and your life: "Follow your heart for success in the coming week."

What a powerful affirmation! What a beautiful reminder of the wisdom that resides within each and every one of us—the wisdom of our hearts, our intuition, and our deepest desires. In a world that often values logic, reason, and practicality above all else, it's easy to forget the importance of tuning in to the whispers of our hearts and allowing them to guide us towards our truest aspirations.

But here's the truth: your heart knows the way. It knows what brings you joy, what ignites your passion, and what fills your soul with a sense of purpose and fulfillment. And when you have the courage to follow its guidance, success—however you define it—is sure to follow.

Following your heart isn't just about pursuing your dreams or achieving your goals—it's about living a life that is aligned with your truest values, passions, and aspirations. It's about honoring your authenticity, embracing your uniqueness, and trusting in the path that unfolds before you, even when it diverges from the expectations of others.

So why follow your heart for success in the coming week? Because when you do, you tap into a wellspring of inspiration, creativity, and resilience that empowers you to overcome any obstacle, navigate any challenge, and seize every opportunity that comes your way.

But following your heart isn't always easy—it requires courage, vulnerability, and a willingness to let go of the need for certainty and control. It means stepping outside your comfort zone, embracing the unknown, and trusting in the journey, even when the path ahead seems unclear.

So as you embark upon the week ahead, I encourage you to heed this powerful affirmation: "Follow your heart for success in the coming week." Let it be your guiding light, your North Star, as you navigate the highs and lows of the days ahead. Let it inspire you to listen to the whispers of your heart, to trust in your intuition, and to embrace the possibilities that lie on the horizon.

Thank you, dear reader, for your willingness to embark on this journey of self-discovery, growth, and transformation. And may your week be filled with moments of joy, inspiration, and success as you follow your heart towards a future filled with abundance, fulfillment, and purpose.

Thank you, and may you have a truly successful week ahead, guided by the wisdom of your heart.

Lucky Numbers 55, 39, 7, 17, 5, 49

81

The evening

The evening promises romantic interests.

Dear readers of "Fortune Cookie Coaching,"

As we delve into the mysteries and wonders of the week ahead, I am thrilled to share with you a message of anticipation, excitement, and the promise of new connections: "The evening promises romantic interests."

What a delightful affirmation! What a beautiful reminder that love, romance, and connection are not just reserved for special occasions or fleeting moments, but are woven into the very fabric of our everyday lives. In a world that can sometimes feel chaotic and uncertain, there is something truly magical about the prospect of kindling romantic interests under the starlit sky of an evening.

But here's the beauty of it: romance isn't just about grand gestures or fairy-tale endings—it's about the little moments, the stolen glances, and the shared laughter that bring color and warmth to our lives. It's about opening our hearts to the possibility of love, embracing the vulnerability of connection, and allowing ourselves to be swept away by the sweet whispers of affection.

So why embrace the promise of romantic interests in the evening? Because in the twilight hours, under the soft glow of moonlight, there is a sense of possibility, of serendipity, and of endless potential that can ignite the flames of passion and awaken the deepest desires of our hearts.

But romantic interests aren't just about finding a partner—they're also about cultivating a sense of romance within ourselves, about nurturing the spark of passion and desire that resides within each and every one of us. It's about falling in love with life, with ourselves, and with the world around us, and allowing that love to radiate outwards, touching the hearts of those we encounter along the way.

So as you embrace the week ahead, I encourage you to open your heart to the promise of romantic interests in the evening. Let it be a reminder to savor the beauty of the present moment, to cherish the connections you share with others, and to allow yourself to be swept away by the magic of love in all its forms.

Thank you, dear reader, for your willingness to embrace the beauty and wonder of romance in the evening. And may your week be filled with moments of love, connection, and unforgettable experiences that leave your heart brimming with joy and gratitude.

Thank you, and may your evenings be filled with the promise of romantic interests that light up your life and fill your heart with love.

LEARN CHINESE - Egg

鸡(jī)蛋(dàn)

Lucky Numbers 3, 36, 47, 38, 52, 56

82

Good luck

You will have good luck in your personal affairs this month.

Dear readers of "Fortune Cookie Coaching,"

As we stand on the threshold of a new month, I am filled with excitement and anticipation for the journey that lies ahead. Within the pages of this transformative book, you've encountered a phrase that holds the promise of abundance, opportunity, and blessings in your personal affairs: "You will have good luck in your personal affairs this month."

What a delightful affirmation! What a beautiful reminder that the universe is conspiring in your favor, aligning the stars and paving the way for success, happiness, and fulfillment in the realm of your personal life. In a world that can sometimes feel chaotic and unpredictable, there is something truly magical about the prospect of good luck shining down upon us, guiding our steps and illuminating our path.

But here's the thing about good luck—it's not just about chance or happenstance. It's about being open to receiving the blessings that come our way, recognizing the opportunities that present themselves, and taking inspired action to make the most of them. It's about cultivating a mindset of abundance, gratitude, and positivity, and trusting in the inherent goodness of the universe to guide us towards our highest good.

So why embrace the promise of good luck in your personal affairs this month? Because in every moment, in every interaction, there is an opportunity for growth, for connection, and for the deepening of our relationships with ourselves and others. Whether it's finding love, strengthening bonds with loved ones, or embarking on a journey of self-discovery, this month holds the promise of miracles and blessings beyond your wildest dreams.

But good luck isn't just about external circumstances—it's also about the choices we make, the actions we take, and the energy we bring to every situation. It's about cultivating a sense of positivity, resilience, and unwavering faith in the face of challenges, setbacks, and obstacles that may arise along the way.

So as you step into the month ahead, I encourage you to embrace the promise of good luck in your personal affairs. Let it be a reminder to approach each day with an open heart and an open mind, to seize every opportunity that comes your way, and to trust in the divine guidance that is leading you towards a future filled with joy, abundance, and fulfillment.

Thank you, dear reader, for your willingness to embrace the magic and wonder of good luck in your personal affairs this month. And may your journey be filled with blessings, miracles, and moments of pure joy and gratitude.

Thank you, and may this month be a time of abundance, prosperity, and incredible blessings in every area of your life.

Lucky Numbers 34, 56, 8, 17, 7, 1

83

You are beautiful

☺ Your are beautiful in and out. People see this. ☺
14 19 32 40 47 6

Dear readers of "Fortune Cookie Coaching,"
Today, I want to remind you of a profound truth—one that resonates deep within each and every one of us: "You are beautiful in and out. People see this."

What a powerful affirmation! What a beautiful reminder of the inherent worth, the unique radiance, and the boundless beauty that resides within you. In a world that often measures beauty by external standards or superficial appearances, it's easy to forget the depth and richness of the beauty that shines from within—the beauty of your spirit, your character, and your essence.

But here's the truth: you are a masterpiece, a work of art, a reflection of the divine. Your beauty transcends physical appearance—it emanates from the depths of your soul, radiating outwards and touching the hearts of everyone you encounter. It's in the kindness of your smile, the warmth of your laughter, and the compassion in your eyes that people see and are drawn to.

So why is it important to recognize and embrace your inner and outer beauty? Because when you do, you step into your power, your authenticity, and your truest essence. You begin to see yourself through the eyes of love and compassion, recognizing the unique gifts and talents that you bring to the world, and honoring the beauty that makes you who you are.

But embracing your beauty isn't just about self-love—it's also about shining your light for others to see, inspiring them to recognize and celebrate their own beauty and worthiness. It's about creating a ripple effect of positivity, kindness, and empowerment that uplifts and transforms the world around you.

So as you continue your journey through the pages of "Fortune Cookie Coaching," I encourage you to hold onto this powerful affirmation: "You are beautiful in and out. People see this." Let it be a reminder to embrace your uniqueness, to honor your worth, and to celebrate the beauty that makes you who you are.

Thank you, dear reader, for your willingness to embrace and celebrate your inner and outer beauty. And may you continue to shine your light bright, illuminating the world with your radiant presence and inspiring others to see and celebrate the beauty within themselves.

Thank you, and may your journey be filled with endless opportunities to embrace and celebrate your inner and outer beauty, spreading love, light, and joy wherever you go.

84

Be what you are

> Do not wish to be anything but what you are, and try to be that perfectly.

Dear readers of "Fortune Cookie Coaching,"

Today, I want to share with you a powerful message—a truth that has the potential to transform your life and set you on a path towards profound fulfillment and authenticity: "Do not wish to be anything but what you are, and try to be that perfectly."

What a profound affirmation! What a beautiful reminder that true happiness, true fulfillment, and true success come from embracing and honoring the unique essence of who you are. In a world that often tells us we need to be more, do more, and achieve more in order to be worthy or valuable, it's easy to lose sight of the beauty and power that resides within our own authenticity.

But here's the truth: you are already perfect, exactly as you are. You are a masterpiece, a one-of-a-kind expression of life's infinite creativity, and there is no one else in the world who can offer what you have to offer. Your quirks, your imperfections, your strengths, and your vulnerabilities—all of it makes you uniquely beautiful and uniquely you.

So why is it important to embrace and embody your true self? Because when you do, you step into your power, your authenticity, and your highest potential. You no longer waste time and energy trying to be someone you're not or living up to someone else's expectations. Instead, you embrace your true essence, your true passions, and your true purpose, and you shine your light brightly for the world to see.

But embracing your true self isn't always easy—it requires courage, vulnerability, and a willingness to let go of the need for approval or validation from others. It means trusting in your own intuition, your own values, and your own unique path, even when it diverges from the expectations of society or those around you.

So as you continue your journey through the pages of "Fortune Cookie Coaching," I encourage you to hold onto this powerful affirmation: "Do not wish to be anything but what you are, and try to be that perfectly." Let it be a reminder to embrace your authenticity, to honor your truth, and to live your life with unwavering integrity and purpose.

Thank you, dear reader, for your willingness to embrace and celebrate your true self. And may you continue to shine your light brightly, inspiring others to do the same and creating a world that celebrates and honors the beauty of authenticity in all its forms.

Thank you, and may your journey be filled with endless opportunities to embrace and embody your true self, living a life of joy, fulfillment, and purpose.

LEARN CHINESE - Orange

橙(chéng)子(zi)

Lucky Numbers 41, 36, 6, 14, 44, 2

85

Happiness

Don't pursue happiness - create it.

Dear readers of "Fortune Cookie Coaching,"

Today, I stand before you with a message that has the power to transform your life—a simple yet profound truth that holds the key to unlocking boundless joy, fulfillment, and meaning: "Don't pursue happiness, create it."

What a powerful affirmation! What a beautiful reminder that happiness is not something we find outside of ourselves, but rather something we cultivate from within. In a world that often tells us happiness is something to be chased, achieved, or acquired through external means, it's easy to lose sight of the fact that true happiness comes from within—from the choices we make, the perspectives we hold, and the actions we take each and every day.

So why is it important to shift from pursuing happiness to creating it? Because when we recognize that happiness is a choice—a state of being that we have the power to cultivate in every moment—we reclaim our agency, our power, and our ability to live a life of joy and fulfillment, regardless of our external circumstances.

Creating happiness is about embracing the present moment, finding gratitude for the blessings in our lives, and choosing to focus on what brings us joy, meaning, and fulfillment. It's about cultivating a mindset of abundance, positivity, and resilience, and trusting in our own ability to navigate life's ups and downs with grace and gratitude.

But creating happiness is also about taking intentional action to align our lives with our deepest values, passions, and aspirations. It's about pursuing activities that light us up, nurturing relationships that bring us joy, and living in alignment with our truest selves. It's about recognizing that happiness is not a destination to be reached, but rather a journey to be embraced—a journey that unfolds moment by moment, choice by choice, and action by action.

So as you continue your journey through the pages of "Fortune Cookie Coaching," I encourage you to hold onto this powerful affirmation: "Don't pursue happiness, create it." Let it be a guiding principle in your life—a reminder to embrace the present moment, cultivate gratitude, and take intentional action to create a life filled with joy, meaning, and fulfillment.

Thank you, dear reader, for your willingness to embrace the power of creating happiness in your life. And may you continue to cultivate joy, gratitude, and fulfillment in every moment, creating a life that reflects the beauty and abundance of your truest self.

Thank you, and may your journey be filled with endless opportunities to create happiness, spread joy, and live a life that truly lights you up from within.

Lucky Numbers 34, 28, 19, 43, 41, 7

86

Financial life

Your financial life will be secure and beneficial.

F ortune Cookie Fam, gather close! We've all cracked open a fortune cookie, read that sweet little message, and maybe even tucked it away with a hopeful smile. But today, let's focus on a particularly powerful phrase: **"Your financial life will be secure and beneficial."**

Now, this isn't some mystical prophecy. It's a **call to action** disguised in a crumbly treat! Let's be honest, financial security isn't about waiting for a lucky break. It's about taking control, making smart choices, and building a foundation that empowers you.

Think about it - financial security isn't just about numbers in a bank account. It's about **peace of mind**. It's the freedom to pursue your dreams, say "yes" to experiences, and weather life's storms without constant worry. It's also about **abundance**. It's having the resources to not just survive, but to thrive, to give back, and to create a life that's truly fulfilling.

Here's the good news - YOU have the power to make this fortune your reality! Remember, this book - Fortune Cookie Coaching - is filled with

FINANCIAL LIFE

actionable steps and wise insights to get you started. Here are some key ingredients for your financial security recipe:

- **Knowledge is power:** Educate yourself on budgeting, saving, and investing.
- **Take control:** Set financial goals, track your spending, and create a plan.
- **Discipline is your friend:** Make consistent choices that prioritize your financial well-being.
- **Embrace delayed gratification:** Short-term sacrifices can lead to long-term gains.

But remember, it's not just about the destination; it's about the journey. There will be setbacks, there will be temptations, but don't let them derail you. Pick yourself up, dust yourself off, and keep moving forward.

And here's the secret sauce: **make it fun!** Challenge yourself, celebrate your wins, and find ways to make financial planning a rewarding adventure.

This fortune may be short and sweet, but its message is powerful: **your financial future can be secure and beneficial.** With the right mindset, the tools from this book, and a sprinkle of Fortune Cookie wisdom, you can make it happen. Believe in yourself, take action, and watch your financial security blossom! Remember, fortune favors the bold – go forth and **build the financial life you deserve!**.

LEARN CHINESE - To cough

咳(ké)嗽(sòu)

Lucky Numbers 50, 8, 30, 6, 40, 37

87

Convictions

You have firm convictions - stand strong behind them.

Fortune Cookie Fam, assemble! Let's crack open another bit of wisdom baked into today's message: **"You have firm convictions, stand strong behind them."** This isn't just about having a stubborn streak – it's about knowing your values, believing in your principles, and having the courage to stand your ground.

Now, life throws plenty of curveballs. There will be times when people question your beliefs, try to sway you from your path, or even mock your convictions. Here's the thing: their opinions don't define you. **Your convictions are your compass**, guiding you towards a life that feels authentic and fulfilling.

Think about it - when you stand strong in your beliefs, you **project confidence**. People are drawn to those who know what they stand for. It fosters respect, attracts like-minded individuals, and empowers you to make decisions that align with your core values.

But holding firm doesn't mean being inflexible. True strength lies in the

CONVICTIONS

ability to **listen with an open mind** while staying true to your core. It's about understanding different perspectives without compromising your own.

Here's how to unlock the power of this fortune:

- **Know your non-negotiables:** What are the values you absolutely will not compromise on?
- **Educate yourself:** Having well-reasoned arguments strengthens your convictions.
- **Learn to communicate effectively:** Express your beliefs clearly and calmly.
- **Be open to respectful discussions:** Listen actively, but stay true to your core.
- **Surround yourself with like-minded people:** A supportive community strengthens your resolve.

Remember, Fortune Cookie Coaching is your guide on this journey. Use the tools in this book to build self-awareness, develop your communication skills, and cultivate unwavering confidence.

Standing firm in your convictions doesn't mean being rigid. It's about **owning your truth**, navigating the world with authenticity, and inspiring others to do the same. So, Fortune Cookie Fam, embrace your convictions, hold your head high, and be the voice you believe in! Remember, the world needs people with unwavering principles, and you are one of them. **Go forth and light the way!.**

9 12 17 18 44 48

Lucky numbers

88

Influential people

The respect of influential people will soon be yours.

Ladies and gentlemen, esteemed readers of "Fortune Cookie Coaching,"

Today, I stand before you to share a profound truth—one that can transform your life, elevate your influence, and open doors you never thought possible. It's encapsulated in a simple yet powerful phrase: **"The respect of influential people will soon be yours."**

Let's dissect this wisdom together:

1. **Self-Respect**: Before seeking the respect of others, cultivate self-respect. Understand your worth, embrace your uniqueness, and honor your journey. When you respect yourself, you radiate confidence, authenticity, and magnetism.
2. **Character Matters**: Influence isn't about popularity; it's about character. Your actions, integrity, and consistency define you. Be deliberate in your choices, for they shape your reputation. As Bruce Lee wisely said, "Knowledge will give you power, but character respect."

3. **Golden Rule**: Treat others as you wish to be treated. Whether you're dealing with a janitor or a CEO, extend kindness, empathy, and genuine interest. Albert Einstein's words resonate: "I speak to everyone in the same way, whether he is the garbage man or the president of the university."
4. **Listen Intently**: One of the sincerest forms of respect is active listening. When you truly hear someone, you honor their thoughts and feelings. Bryant H. McGill reminds us, "Never judge someone by the way he looks or a book by the way it's covered; for inside those tattered pages, there's a lot to be discovered."
5. **Elevate Others**: Lift people up. Acknowledge their contributions, celebrate their successes, and offer encouragement. Thomas S. Monson wisely said, "When we treat people as if they were what they should be, they will become what they should be."
6. **Choose Integrity**: William J. H. Boetcker's words resonate: "That you may retain your self-respect, it is better to displease the people by doing what you know is right than to temporarily please them by doing what you know is wrong."
7. **Lead by Example**: Influence isn't about titles; it's about impact. Lead with authenticity, humility, and vision. Your actions ripple through your team, your community, and beyond.
8. **Build Bridges**: Respect bridges gaps. Seek common ground, appreciate diversity, and build connections. As Confucius wisely said, "Without feelings of respect, what is there to distinguish men from beasts?"
9. **Gratitude**: Express gratitude sincerely. Thank those who've influenced you, mentored you, or stood by your side. Gratitude fosters respect and deepens relationships.
10. **Legacy**: Remember that your legacy isn't measured by wealth or fame. It's the positive impact you leave behind—the lives you've touched, the kindness you've shown, and the respect you've earned.

In conclusion, dear readers, embrace this truth: The respect of influential people isn't an elusive dream; it's within your grasp. Live with purpose,

lead with integrity, and watch as doors swing open, revealing a world of possibilities.

"*Respect yourself and others will respect you.*" – Confucius

Thank you, and may your journey be filled with respect, influence, and unwavering purpose. ✨

LEARN CHINESE - Today

今(jīn)天(tiān)

Lucky Numbers 45, 37, 51, 15, 14, 47

About the Author

Defined by Nature: Planet Earth Inhabitant, Human, Son of Eladio Rodulfo & Briceida Moya, Brother of Gabriela, Gustavo & Katiuska, Father of Gabriel & Sofia; **Defined by the Society**: Venezuelan Citizen (*Human Rights Limited by default*), Friend of many, Enemy of few, Neighbor, Student/Teacher/Student, Worker/Supervisor/Manager/Leader/Worker, Husband of Katty/ Ex-Husband of K/Husband of Yohana; **Defined by the US Immigration System**: Legal Alien; **Defined by the Gig Economy**: Independent Contractor Form 1099; **Studies in classroom**: Master Degree in Human Resources Management, English, Chinese Mandarin, Part 107 Drone Operator; **Studies at the real world**: Human Behavior; **Studies at home**: Webmaster SEO, Graphic Web Apps Design, Internet & Social Media Marketing, Video Production, You Tube Branding, Trading, Import-Exports, Affiliate Marketing, Cooking, Laundry, Home Cleaning; **Work experience**: Public-Private-Entrepreneur Sectors; **Other Definitions**: Bitcoin Evangelist, Human Rights Peace and Love Advocate; **Author of**: Why Maslow: How to use his theory to stay in Power Forever (EN/SP); Asylum Seekers (EN/SP); Manual for Gorillas: 9 Rules to be the "*Fer-pect*" Dictator (EN/SP); Why you must Play the Lottery (EN/SP); Para Español Oprima #2: Speaking Spanish in Times of Xenophobia (EN/SP), Cause of Death: IGNORANCE | Human Behavior in Times of PANIC (SP/EN); Left Right Politics explained for Millennials Gens XYZ and next generations

(SP/EN) | Las cenizas del Ejército Libertador (SP/EN); Remain Silent, the only right we have. The legal aliens (SP/EN) **Host of the YouTube Channel & Podcast: Ubuntu Cafe (ubuntu.cafe)**; Producer of the Podcast: Vicky Erotic Tales and All Books.

You can connect with me on:
- https://juanrodulfo.com
- https://twitter.com/rodulfox
- https://facebook.com/rodulfox
- https://g.co/kgs/grjtN5
- https://www.linkedin.com/in/rodulfox
- http://bit.ly/3J8rbUP

Subscribe to my newsletter:
- https://juanrodulfo.com

Also by Juan Rodulfo

Watching humans hit the same stone again and again

Remain Silent: The only right we have. The legal Aliens
https://juanrodulfo.com
According to Manuel Lopez Obrador, Mexico president, 10.000 migrants go to the US border a day, most of this humans are apprehended by ICE, stripped of all their belongings, sometimes violating their Human Rights, sent to Detention Centers and held in these centers, for days or months, to be released most of them with orders to appear in Immigration Courts, some of them are released with ankle monitors, some of them are released with a cellphone in both cases to be monitored 24/7.

www.ingramcontent.com/pod-product-compliance
Lightning Source LLC
LaVergne TN
LVHW021957060526
838201LV00048B/1603